ANTHROPOSOPHY (A FRAGMENT)

ANTHROPOSOPHY
(A FRAGMENT)

RUDOLF STEINER

A New Foundation for the Study of Human Nature

Translated by CATHERINE E. CREEGER
and DETLEF HARDORP

🌿 ANTHROPOSOPHIC PRESS

The original German text is published under the title *Anthroposophie: Ein Fragment aus dem Jahre 1910* (Vol. 45 in the Bibliographic Survey) by the Rudolf Steiner Nachlassverwaltung, Dornach, 1970.

Published by Anthroposophic Press, Inc.
RR 4, Box 94 A-1, Hudson, N.Y. 12534

Library of Congress Cataloging-in-Publication Data

Steiner, Rudolf, 1861–1925.
   [Anthroposophie (1910). English]
   Anthroposophy (a fragment) / Rudolf Steiner ; translated by
Catherine E. Creeger and Detlef Hardorp.
    p. cm. — (Classics in anthroposophy)
   Includes bibliographical references and index.
   ISBN 0-88010-401-5 (pbk.)
   1. Anthroposophy. I. Title. II. Series.
BP595.S894A5713   1995
299'.935—dc20   95-21414
                                     CIP

Cover painting and design: Barbara Richey

10 9 8 7 6 5 4 3 2 1

Printed in the United States of America

CONTENTS

Dr. James Dyson

It is perhaps significant that this first English edition of *Anthroposophy (A Fragment)* has awaited publication for so long. Eighty-five years have elapsed since it was written, encompassing virtually a century of unprecedented scientific and technological developments. Its content is interdisciplinary—essentially an attempt to address, through cognitive science, subjects that would at the present time be classified as developmental neuro-sensory psychology and neuro-physiology. Since it was written, these disciplines have seen developments as radical as those in nuclear physics, genetics, or immunology, and research methodology has entered a new era of technological possibilities.

What relevance, then, can an eighty-five-year-old unfinished document such as this have for the present? Ultimately, the question can be answered only by the reader and by the test of time. Nevertheless, convinced that the neuro-sciences have needed the intervening decades to catch up with Steiner, I have responded positively to the publisher's request to write an introduction.

Although this last statement may sound extreme, I shall try in what follows to point to a number of developments in neurology and psychology that have taken place since Steiner's time and that support the view that this "Fragment" is particularly timely today.

First, however, I will give a brief biographical introduction to Steiner himself, as his work is generally not as well known in the English-speaking world as it has become in central Europe.

An Austrian-born philosopher and cognitive scientist, Rudolf Steiner (1861–1925) embarked on his own path of research at a very young age. As a child, he felt painfully isolated from other people. Not only did he experience, like everyone else, the world of sense-perceptions and the ideas related to them, but he was also aware of an inner dimension of experience not based on sense perception at all. He later used the terms "the sense world" and "the spiritual world" to describe these two dimensions. During his adolescence, he set himself the task of understanding how these two worlds were connected, in terms of cognitive science and philosophy. While pursuing this task as a young university student, he became committed to making the results of his research generally available in the prevailing language of his day. He was convinced that, if it was presented in the right way, it would be understandable on its own terms and would not have to rely on any presumed system of spiritual or religious belief for its validation.

His main subjects of study were philosophy, mathematics, and natural science. Since the days of Isaac Newton, these disciplines have been based upon a methodology of reductionism. Essentially, reductionism endeavors to understand the whole as a function of its constituent parts, which, in turn, are subjected to quantitative analysis. By concentrating only on the weighable and measurable, the reductionist researcher increasingly excludes from consideration the qualitative aspects of sense-perceptions—these being regarded as subjective and outside the field of proper scientific inquiry.

Steiner soon recognized a different research methodology in Johann Wolfgang von Goethe's approach to such diverse subjects as botany and color; and, as he deepened his understanding of this, he became convinced that he had found the key to the problem of how to connect his two worlds of experience. In contrast to reductionism, Goethe's methodology regards the qualitative experience of nature to be a primary perception as much as the quantitative—not just a subjective elaboration of the latter. Goethe was convinced that qualitative perception could be raised to the level of objectivity through training a faculty, which nowadays could be termed *deductive intuition*. According to this method, the part can only be understood in its relation to the whole. This approach is outlined in depth in *Goethe's Scientific Consciousness* by Henri Bortoft.[1]

In his *The Metamorphosis of Plants*, Goethe endeavored to lay the foundations for a new natural science of the organic world.[2] Steiner, who at the age of twenty-one had accepted an invitation to edit the scientific writings in the Centenary Goethe-edition, published a commentary and interpretation of Goethe's methodology as an introduction.[3] This he later elaborated in the book *A Theory of*

Knowledge Implicit in Goethe's World Conception.[4] In this work Steiner made his own original contribution to the field of cognitive science. The full implications of his thesis did not, however, make the impact on the prevailing trends of late nineteenth century thought that he had hoped for.

Subsequently, at the age of thirty-three, Steiner wrote his main philosophical work, now published in English under the title *Intuitive Thinking as a Spiritual Path: A Philosophy of Freedom*.[5] This was an elaboration of his doctoral thesis, which had been accepted by Rostock University some years earlier.[6] In his thesis, Steiner set out to refute the Kantian view that our sense perceptions, due to their inherently subjective nature, can never be relied upon as objective instruments of truth. Steiner countered this stance by describing how our mental pictures of the outside world arise from two sides: one via pure sense-perception (originating in the outer world) and the other via an inner activity through which the sense-perception becomes recognizable and can be interpreted (corresponding to deductive intuition).

According to Steiner, human beings have the unique possibility to integrate these two processes and, thus, to participate in building their own *reality* of ideation. He also makes the further proposition that the integration of the apparently separate inner and outer worlds, which takes place during the course of childhood and adolescence, provides the basis for the later development of the faculty of free will. He called this latent faculty *moral intuition*.

Steiner also outlined a discipline of cognitive training through which powers of observation can be refined and extended to include not only the outer aspects of the sense-perceptible world but also the way in which we ourselves contribute to the act of cognition—that is, through feelings and unconscious recognition patterns. His thesis culminated in the proposition that in every act of cognition we have the possibility of extending the boundaries of our freedom and thereby also our personal responsibility. His ultimate definition of a free individuality was that of "a person who can will what one, as an individual, believes to be right."

Shortly after completing *Intuitive Thinking: A Philosophy of Freedom* in 1894, Steiner's activities were increasingly diverted away from academic life. He admitted to being profoundly disappointed that neither his philosophical nor his scientific contemporaries really understood what he was saying or, if they did, that they did not see it as having any great significance. While continuing to avail himself of those opportunities life offered him to enter the general scientific and cultural debates of his day, he found a more understanding audience in the Theosophical Society. He collaborated with them from the turn of the century till 1913, when he ended this association because his views regarding the nature of Christianity differed fundamentally from those of the Theosophists. From the beginning, Steiner's association with Theosophy had been something of an uneasy alliance, but it was an important part of his destiny, through which he found the platform and support he needed to continue his work as a lecturer and writer. During this period (1901–1913), he concentrated on the elaboration of the results of his own spiritual research,[7] whereas previously he had confined himself primarily to describing its methodological basis.

From 1902 onward, Steiner began to use the term *Anthroposophy* to describe both the results of his spiritual research and the methods by which it was achieved. As time went on he increasingly distinguished the meaning of this term from that of Theosophy, as he elaborates in the first chapter of *Anthroposophy (A Fragment)*.

Steiner's sojourn in the Theosophical movement meant of necessity that initially he adopted Eastern terminology to describe the results of his own research. He saw Anthroposophy, however, as essentially growing from a Western tradition. He hoped to be able to show how it could be developed directly from the stream of Western thinking that had, in his view, reached its pinnacle in Goethe's scientific work. For he was convinced that a true science of the sense world could lead naturally to a science of the spiritual world. Throughout his life, he maintained that spiritual research in its methodology was not fundamentally different from scientific research, provided that the latter did not exclude the observer from the field of inquiry—that is, that the research was not reductionist. It was particularly with this aim that Steiner began writing this *Fragment*.

Despite his commitment to this goal, he was not able to complete the task. In the publisher's foreword to the 1970 German edition, which is included in this translation, the editors have printed extracts from two of Steiner's lectures, in which he describes in a remarkably frank and detailed way some of the difficulties that presented themselves while he was working on this book, and why they obstructed its progress, preventing its final completion. He frequently refers to the fact "that the language needed to give his thoughts clear expression was not available at that time."

It would not impose too narrow an interpretation on this remark to say that it suggests the neurosciences had not yet progressed sufficiently for his purpose. In reading the *Fragment* one can clearly recognize Steiner's commitment to linking his own insights with the findings already made in this field. If his success in achieving this only appears to have been partial, we may perhaps recognize this as inevitable, when viewed in the context of the extremely limited scientific knowledge at his disposal. After all, only the most elementary experiments on the nervous system had been performed when this *Fragment* was being written. Nevertheless, the conclusions drawn from them were so powerful that they still form the foundations of contemporary physiology.

. . . . . .

These experiments take as their starting point the investigation of reflex movement and are usually carried out on the limb of a frog from which the cerebrum has been removed. An external stimulus is applied, usually in the form of an electric current, and one is able to observe the response in the form of a jerk in the limb. Dissection and histological study of the tissues show that reflex movements of this kind are sustained in their most simple form through the presence of essentially two nerve cells, with a junction (synapse) between them within the central nervous system. One cell conveys the stimulus toward the nervous system, and the other away from it in the form of a trigger reaction.

The concept of the spinal reflex arc has evolved from this simple and easily repeatable experiment. The afferent nerve conveying the stimulus from the outside world has been denoted as *sensory,* and its partner or efferent nerve has been denoted as *motor*. This model has paved the way for the development of a theory of brain function based on cause and effect. Although the complexities of neuroanatomy now describe an almost infinite number of ways in which this basic spinal reflex can be modified, reinforced, or inhibited by stimuli coming from higher centers in the brain, the basic notion that the nervous system is explicable in terms of this simple input/output model has prevailed.

One can easily appreciate why it is that this attractive hypothesis has had such a compellingly powerful influence on the interpretation of the neurological basis of both movement and cognition. Whether the last word has been spoken on the subject—even in such a narrowly defined area as that of the spinal reflex arc—is still questionable. What is clear, however, is that the gulf between the subject of reflex movement on the one hand, and the science of cognition and sense-perception on the other, is an enormous one by any standard. Despite the obvious dangers of applying the basic principles of the former field of study to the latter, most authors continue to attempt just this. However understandable this may be— for to propose alternative explanations would require radical thinking which, with its attendant absence of traditional boundaries, demands considerable inner courage— to be misled at this very point has far-reaching consequences for an understanding of the physiological basis of consciousness and all of its attendant implications.

The development of computer science and technology has successfully reinforced the *instructionist* model of the nervous system, which is based on the concept of data processing. The argument goes that computers can be explained using the same "building-block" principles that apparently exist in the reflex arc. They also share the need for external stimulation to generate meaningful activity— both require "instruction." Whereas the entire working of even the most sophisticated computer can be shown to conform to this model, a similar mechanism operating in the human brain is merely assumed.[8]

Because this instructionist model is externally determined and driven, a compatible psychology of the mind would in turn need to identify the source of any apparent sense of subjective meaning or motivation outside the human being. The behavioral school of psychology— originally founded early in this century by J. B. Watson and I. P. Pavlov, and reaching the height of its influence with B. F. Skinner and others in the 1960s and 1970s[9]— met these requirements perfectly. Perhaps behaviorism's greatest single effect has been to undermine the assumption that each one of us has some access to an independent conscience and thereby to free moral choice. According to the behavioral paradigm, ultimately we are not answerable to anyone, because we are all subject to a behavioristic program. Based on experiments with pigeons and rats and their response to rewards—usually in the form of food—this school of thought ultimately demotes personal views, attitudes, and convictions to the level of complex conditioned reflexes, which arise as a consequence of information processing. Here, the computer analogy is at work once again. The one basic drive we are still allowed to own is the desire for the gratification of basic bodily instincts, and even this drive is presumed to have been programmed into us for some survivalist purpose.

Behavioristic interpretations allow little or no place for the notion of individual freedom or morality, which do not, it is said, fall within the scope of scientific inquiry. Science is, after all, concerned with the objective world; experiences such as conscience, being merely subjective, are, in the final analysis, illusory! Reductionism thereby reveals its devious strategy. First, it undermines confidence in the inner power of judgment, and then it replaces this with the assumption that the human being is simply an animal endowed with a particularly advanced form of computer program.

Naturally, this shift of fundamental orientation has had—and is still having—far-reaching consequences, both for how people view their relationships to one another and the consequent effects on general attitudes in society. On the one hand, we have experienced a loss of respect for traditional values, as witnessed by increased cynicism, opportunism, and crime; on the other hand, there is the loss of a sense of meaning and motivation, leading to lethargy and detachment. Its impact on educational philosophy and psychology, and the resulting influences on methods of teaching and examinations, both among children and adults, is beyond estimation, as is the effect of these very methods on the physiological and psychological integrity of developing human beings. Its consequences for medical practice have been at least as monumental.

During the course of the twentieth century, and especially since the Second World War, humanistic and existentialist schools of psychology have emerged. These have an orientation fundamentally different from behaviorism. One of the first to gain ground was Gestalt psychology, founded in the 1930s by M. Wertheimer, W. Kohler, and K. Koffka and subsequently developed by Fritz Perls in the 1960s as Gestalt therapy.[10] Gestalt psychology began by studying the way in which perception is influenced by the context or configuration of the elements perceived—that is, the content of the world does not meet us in a readymade form. As a therapy, this approach stresses that a person's own needs form an integral part of the needs of the world and vice versa; furthermore, the relationship of the individual to the world requires the will to confront unpleasant experiences as well as ones which offer immediate gratification. If the path of pain-avoidance is taken, the individual thereby breaks the "Gestalt" in his or her

unique relationship to the world. This approach emphasizes the importance of cultivating the ability to live in the
present moment, through which the individual may realize
his or her unique potential for self-determination. A
closely related approach is Psychosynthesis, founded by
the Italian psychologist Roberto Assagioli, author of the
book *The Human Will*.[11]

These therapies blazed a new trail in the 1950s and
onward, providing a welcome alternative to behaviorism,
which was championed by B. F. Skinner at that time and
a little later, by the zoologist Desmond Morris, author of
The Naked Ape; they are well remembered for their keen
enthusiasm for rats and chimpanzees, respectively.

In the last decade, largely through his two books, *The
Road Less Traveled* and *People of the Lie*, M. Scott Peck
has found a very wide general readership, presenting a
convincing case for the examination of the principles of
Good and Evil as primary entities in the disciplines of psychology and psychiatry.[12] He argues that for too long these
subjects have been dismissed, simply because they belong
to the seemingly subjective realm. In fact, this fundamental challenge to one of science's most entrenched tenets
was prefigured in the 1960s by the psychologist Rollo
May. May achieved considerable influence, particularly
through his comprehensive book *Love and Will*, in which
he substantiates the proposition that love has more to do
with integrity than the pursuit of the pleasure principle—a
radical counterblow to behaviorism.[13]

In fact, much of what emerged in existentialist and
humanistic psychology was in some respects prefigured

in the development of the Viennese school of psychoanalytic psychiatry, particularly in the work of Carl Gustav Jung. This was elaborated and further developed by Viktor Frankl, the founder of Logotherapy, who was strongly influenced by his experiences while working with Jewish prisoners in concentration camps. Logotherapy challenges the client to create value as a free inner act amidst a sea of otherwise potential meaningless experiences.[14]

The cumulative effect of the humanistic and existentialist schools has been to open up new and "future-oriented" forms of personal counseling and psychotherapy. (Earlier psychoanalytic practice, largely under the influence of its founder, Sigmund Freud, tended to concentrate more on the past through the interpretation of experiences and traumas of early life. However, these two approaches are by no means mutually exclusive.) Based on the recognition of the potential for growth and development, these schools challenge the individual to develop, as an inner act of free will, latent faculties of self-awareness and thus to assume his or her place within the evolving body of world consciousness. In this way, they stand in sharp contrast to behaviorism, which sees consciousness in terms of biological conditioning.

Notwithstanding their widespread recognition, counseling and psychology have remained rather poorly represented in mainstream psychiatric medicine—at least in Great Britain. Mainly, the latter still tries to uphold the classical basis of biological psychiatry, which seeks to bridge or block key metabolic processes by administering the appropriate drug. Until now, behaviorism has largely held sway in this field, because its *instructionism* merges conveniently with the heritage of classical neurology, which then goes hand-in-hand with the reductionist approach in biological psychiatry.

One of the relatively few people to have publicly wrestled with the limitations of classical neurology in recent decades is Oliver Sacks, himself a neurologist and neuropsychiatrist. Through his brilliant clinical observations, combined with extraordinary human interest and literary ability, he has been able to make the mysterious workings of the senses and the brain accessible to his readers, without imposing on them any personal interpretations. His writings are remarkable in that they engage the interest of both the general readership and the relatively narrow band of professionals researching this field. Anyone who has not already read his works is encouraged to do so— for example: *A Leg to Stand on*; *The Man who Mistook his Wife for a Hat*; *Seeing Voices; Awakenings;* and *An Anthropologist on Mars*. Combining an experience of sheer joy with a wider scientific value, they also assume a special significance in the light of Steiner's writings and lectures on the senses and cognitive science, generally, and, in particular, this *Fragment*.

For decades, existentialist and humanistic psychologies have been seeking for a model of the nervous system as an alternative to that of classical neurology. Without being able to point to sound physiological foundations, they are vulnerable to being "tarred" with the brush of mysticism and, consequently, marginalized by mainstream academic science. Deserving of special attention for the attempt to seek an alternative model is *The Self and Its Brain*, by Carl Popper and Sir John Eccles. This book presents a very different case, based on thorough knowledge, and displaying masterly argumentation. Although it found its way onto the bookshelves of serious students, it did not make the decisive impact in general academics that many felt it warranted; hence, the current excitement around further research, which once again calls into question the *instructionist* model of the nervous system—this time in a very concise and decisive way.

This most recent revolution is being led by Gerald Edelman, a Nobel Prize-winning biologist. A full exposition of his ideas appeared in his book, *Bright Air and Brilliant Fire*.[15] In fact, Edelman and his colleagues had been developing their ideas since the mid-1970s. Moreover, serious students of developmental neurology have witnessed for some time a gulf appearing between neurological theory and cognitive psychology. It must be acknowledged that the neurophysiology of sensory and cognitive psychology has become one of the most specialized branches of the biological sciences, comparable to immunology. The field simply does not lend itself readily to the kind of experimental methods using Ringer's solution and petri dishes, through which the model of the reflex arc was devised in the last century. It is hardly surprising, therefore, to find that Edelman's theory requires more effort to grasp than its forerunners in the field—although, for those with a background in Steiner's theories of cognitive science and developmental psychology, it has a remarkable ring of familiarity.

An entirely new theory is needed, Edelman argues, to explain the origin of individual diversity of perceptions and thoughts; moreover, such a theory could not be based on a mechanistic or computer model but only on a science corresponding to the nature of the *living* world. He is referring to the processes of natural selection as described by Darwin and also to his own discoveries concerning the immune system (for which he received a Nobel Prize in 1972), which have challenged and superseded the idea that the molecular structure of an antigen determines the structure of its corresponding antibody by a simple process analogous to instruction.

He points out that the greatest single flaw in instructionism is that it (unconsciously) presupposes that somewhere out there in the world all manner of objects and interrelationships exist in a neatly labeled fashion, just waiting to be incorporated into the brain. He maintains that the world is, in fact, in its primary state, totally amorphous and chaotic—at least in any functional or cognitive sense—and just doesn't contain neatly organized modules of information. He emphasizes that it is the brain itself that must first generate its own categories before it can begin to process sensory information in terms of concepts, mental images, or judgments. In other words, the way we perceive the outside world depends mainly on the organism which is doing the perceiving—namely, ourselves!

This theory of cognition comes remarkably close to Steiner's. Compare it, for example, with the following quotation from the preface to his book *Truth and Knowledge*:

... The outcome of what follows is that truth is not, as is usually assumed, an ideal reflection of something real, but a product of the human spirit, created by an activity which is free and independent; this product would exist nowhere if we did not create it ourselves. The object of gaining perceptive insight is not to repeat in conceptual form something which already exists, but rather to "create" a completely new sphere which only offers complete reality if seen in conjunction with the world we perceive through the senses. The highest human activity, creative activity of the human mind and spirit, is an organic part of the general progress of the world. Without it, the progress of the world could not be conceived as a whole complete in itself. Human beings are not idle onlookers observing the progress of the world, merely recapitulating in their minds images of events that take place in the cosmos and in which they are not involved. They take an active part in the creation of the world's progress. Perceptive insight is the most perfect thing in the organism of the universe.

The approaches of both Steiner and Edelman emphasize that our experience of the outer world does not reach us in a readymade or predetermined form and that therefore our understanding of the brain ultimately cannot be reduced to the notion of a programmed computer mechanism. They also shed light on some questions in the field of neurophysiology, which the instructionists have generally preferred to avoid. It is estimated for instance that there are approximately 100 billion nerve cells in the central nervous system with some million billion possible interconnections in the brain itself. The number of possible patterns that this ground structure allows for is certainly well beyond the possibility of anything numerically definable; that is to say, it approaches infinity. A key question is, how are these to become defined and channeled? It is difficult from an instructionist viewpoint to visualize a program of sensory input which would, of itself, do anything more than produce a state of sheer cerebral confusion.

In Edelman's theory, this infinite possibility of patterns corresponds to the infinite possibilities of movement and of thought inherent in the brain. According to him, the key to how these are selected lies in the structures located in the brain stem, which he has called "value systems." These have diffuse ramifications throughout the entire cerebral cortex. These are apparently among the most ancient structures in the entire nervous system. Quoting Edelman directly from a BBC "Horizon" documentary, broadcast on January 29, 1994:

> The main idea is that these are ascending diffuse systems that go all over your brain—particularly your cortex—in such a way as to fire when something is salient, when something might have value. They aren't the systems that recognize the difference between a square and a cube, but if particular patterns come up that signal that system, then when

that system fires, neurons that happen to be firing do make the discrimination, and get strengthened rather than weakened; and so, value gets imposed in the brain by the brain. These value systems would seem to retain a primordial imprint of some kind, whereby a specific firing pattern, when standing in a relationship to a sense perception, is somehow recognized as good or appropriate. In such a way this particular firing pattern is strengthened, and in the long run other connections which have not been reinforced retire from active service, and possibly atrophy.

In order to test his theory, Edelman, as Steiner had done before him, carefully studied how children build a cognitive and functional relationship with their environment. Babies display a broad repertoire of undefined possibilities of movement that evolve through different patterns called primitive reflexes, and eventually narrow down to those enabling the growing child to deal most effectively with its immediate environment. That is to say, the baby has a universal potentiality for spontaneous activity, which becomes increasingly confined and defined through its meeting, via the senses, the initially chaotic and amorphous impressions of the environment. Only gradually does the character of these sense impressions become intelligible to the child's developing cognitive understanding.

Edelman postulates that just those patterns of movement proving most helpful to the child are unconsciously selected—hence the parallel with Darwin's theory of natural selection which states that from the multiplicity of possible forms or mutations, only those will emerge that confer some survival advantage on the particular species. However, rather than being survival-oriented, the guiding principle at work in the developing child is her or his evolving interest and motivation. The difference between this theory and that of instructionism will not require further elaboration.

A serious student of Steiner will probably be reminded of his description of how movement, as an expression of the life of will, as such does not originate in the nervous system—the task of which is to provide it with its boundaries—but rather in what he terms the *metabolic system*. This is elaborated in his book *Von Seelenrätseln* (*The Riddles of the Soul*):

> The fact remains that unprejudiced contemplation of the psyche obliges us to recognize the existential independence of the will; and accurate insight into the findings of physiology compels the conclusion that the will as such must be linked not with neural but with metabolic processes. If one wants to form clear concepts in this field, then one must look at the findings of physiology and psychology in the light of the facts themselves and not, as so often happens in the present-day practice of those sciences, in the light of preconceived opinions and definitions, not to mention theoretical sympathies and antipathies.

Most important of all one must be able to discern very clearly the mutual interrelation of neural function, breathing rhythm and metabolic activity respectively. . . . Only materialistic presupposition can relate the element of metabolism in the nerves with the process of ideation. Observation with its roots in reality reports quite differently. It is compelled to recognize that metabolism is present in the nerve to the extent that the will is permeating it.

But in the nerves something else goes on that is quite distinct from metabolism and rhythm. The somatic processes in the nervous system which provide the foundation for representation and ideation are physiologically difficult to grasp. That is because wherever there is neural function, it is accompanied by the ideation which is ordinary consciousness. But the converse of this is also true. Where there is no ideation, there it is never specifically neural function we discern, but only metabolic activity in the nerve, or rhythmic occurrence in it, as the case may be. Neurology will never arrive at concepts that measure up to the facts, so long as it fails to see that the specifically neural activity of the nerve cannot possibly be an object of physiological empirical observation. Anatomy and physiology must bring themselves to recognize that neural function can be located only by a method of exclusion. The activity of the nerves is precisely that in them which is not perceptible to the senses, though the fact that it must be there can be inferred from what is so perceptible, and so can the specific nature of their activity. The only way of representing neural function to ourselves is to see in it those material events, by means of which the purely psycho-spiritual reality of the living content of ideation is subdued and devitalized (*herabgelähmt*) to the lifeless representations and ideas which we recognize as our ordinary consciousness. Unless this concept finds its way somehow into physiology, physiology can have no hope of explicating neural activity.

At present physiology has committed itself to methods that conceal rather than reveal this concept.[16]

The perspectives that emerge from both Steiner and Edelman offer much more than a new explanation of how complex motor skills are acquired. They allow the thought that inherent within human physiology, a deeper form of unconscious *wisdom* may be at work, which in the course of its encounter with sense impressions, contributes to the way in which concepts, mental images, emotions, and judgments are built up. Thereby, everyone acquires a unique relationship to their sense impressions and develops a totally original constellation of inner possibilities for comprehension and creativity. A careful distinction must be made at this point between the *value systems* themselves and what arises from their interaction with sense impressions. Value systems do not, of themselves, confer uniqueness to the human being—they are universal. It is their nature to allow infinite diversity of possible forms of expression to arise, when they are fructified in their interface with sense impressions that confront each individual in a unique complex according to life circumstances.

Expressed in its most basic form, this means t'
individual responds differently to similar types oɪ ᴏᴄ
input—a picture that runs completely counter to the
instructionist or behavioral model.

It may be argued that Edelman's theory only pushes the
frontiers of the inquiry one step back, leaving unad-
dressed how *value* arose within *value systems* in the first
place. This may indeed be the case. But at this point scientific explanation reaches a certain boundary. As science
claims to serve the pursuit of truth, it follows that truth
must always be in harmony with the findings of science.
From this claim, however, it does not follow that the findings of science can prove something true, though often it
is mistakenly assumed to do so. They can only support or
contradict what is, and remains, essentially an act of
deductive intuition. A hypothesis is a deductive intuition
that must either be confirmed or disallowed by the facts.
However, the apparent affirmation of the hypothesis by
facts does not prove the hypothesis, but only allows it to
stand. In the final analysis, all truth is unprovable and can
only be intuitively grasped. This is equally true for both
simple and complex hypotheses—for example, one plus
one makes two. The facts of the outer world support this
intuition but can never prove it; its truth is inherent and
can only be recognized as an inner cognitive act. The
more complex question of whether consciousness, in fact,
created the world, or whether consciousness evolved
from the atom, must ultimately rest on a similar cognitive
act of intuition—albeit, this must also be tested continually against the facts, in so far as they can be investigated.

Steiner was quite clear on this point—from the time of his youth, it was central to his cognitive theories. After he became connected to Theosophy, however, he made the consequences of this stance far more explicit; and his work was based, without reservation, on the premise that any inherent *unconscious* values were originally derived from a form of creative being to which humanity could gradually gain conscious access through a path of spiritual schooling. Along this path described by Steiner, it becomes possible to gradually expand the frontiers of personal freedom, because ultimately one comes into the position of being able to choose how to relate to all aspects of sense impressions—that is, the ultimate potential exists to be free, even in relation to the most basic and immediate sense impressions mediating our contact with so-called outer reality.

Edelman's work clearly begs similar questions of orientation. However, it does not directly challenge us in this way—perhaps wisely so. Instead, the salient issue raised by this work lies in the question as to whether his neuroscientific research will make a lasting impact on mainstream academic thought; if so, will it then be taken up by the closely related applied sciences of clinical psychology and medicine and, ultimately, encapsulated? Even within such a closely related family of disciplines, it does not necessarily follow that a cross-fertilization of insights will automatically occur. How long it will take for the full implications of Edelman's work to filter through into actual practice—assuming they *will* be taken up in their own right—therefore remains a matter of conjecture. The argument that there is a paucity of generalists and a surplus of specialists is well-founded in exactly this domain of research.

Owen Barfield referred to the lack of general recognition of Steiner's work as "one of the academic miracles of the twentieth century." The main reason for this lies most likely in the fact that Steiner was perhaps one of the greatest generalists in modern academic history. It did not seem credible—even in his day when specialization was still in its infancy—that a single individual should claim authority in such apparently diverse subjects as philosophy, natural science, education, medicine, agriculture, architecture, as well as others.

Plausible as this explanation is, however, the noetic issues outlined above have almost certainly been more influential. It is not as if it were simply a question of accepting or rejecting isolated academic theory; the undeniable reality is that from the beginning of his life, Steiner was swimming against the tide of the ingrained reductionist dogma, which implicitly nurtured and guarded a materialistic world-outlook. From the moment that he spoke and wrote openly about the primacy of the creative world of spirit, all materialistically based sciences inevitably assumed their distance from his work, and consequently a kind of conspiracy of silence arose, which is often a more effective form of attack than any argument. Furthermore, when Steiner proceeded to describe the experiences of the human being between death and rebirth—the laws of reincarnation and karma—and the redeeming role of the Christ in Earth evolution, no simple shift of attitude or orientation could ever have changed this tide.

The necessary shift that science would have had to make—at least, in principle—to encompass Steiner's work, would have been of a different magnitude; to use a phrase coined in the New Age movement, it would have required a *paradigm shift* in the prevailing scientific consciousness. In fact, it had always been Steiner's hope that, in the long run, Anthroposophy would pioneer the emergence of just such a shift of consciousness. His warnings about the consequences for humanity, if this fails, were at least as accurate as they then seemed apocalyptic. This is not to imply that Anthroposophy has completely failed its task. However, it cannot be denied that, so far, its influence has fallen far short of its potential within general culture, especially in the English-speaking world.

Most of Steiner's predictions have in fact been born out in the crises currently manifesting in most fields of our cultural life—medicine, education, agriculture, and so on—not to mention the more obvious and increasingly acknowledged ecological and economic catastrophes now threatening Planet Earth on an unprecedented scale. In short, the practical consequences of applied reductionism are finally coming home to roost. Sadly, the forms of thought needed to make this diagnosis—at least in circles potentially influential to the situation—are also those that reductionism has largely succeeded in eroding. This is probably its greatest single triumph. Meanwhile, human civilization will continue to pay the high price of this powerful deception.

It is beyond the scope of this Introduction to do more than touch upon the effect of reductionism in the areas of practical and cultural life, though Steiner devoted the majority of his work during the last seven years of his life to practice in these areas. What is most remarkable about his advice, in all its applications, is its detail and specificity. Steiner was not content to remain in the sphere of spiritual generalizations, but translated spiritual insights into methods to be taken up in the shop.

One example of this can be found in *Anthroposophy (A Fragment)*, which covers the senses and life-processes. These themes have a central role in Steiner's educational philosophy and the resulting approach to teaching that constitutes the so-called Waldorf Curriculum, named after the first school established with Steiner's help in Stuttgart. They have been equally formative in the education of those with special needs, particularly in the founding of the Camphill Movement by Dr. Karl König and his close collaborators. They developed, through their own research, a *diagnostic circle* of twelve senses which has provided—and continues to provide—significant insights into many aspects of learning difficulties, developmental disturbances, and congenital syndromes. This work invites much more widespread research and evaluation; however, this is difficult to follow up without the benefits of mainstream academic and financial resources to draw upon. Were this to be undertaken, a new surge of interest in Steiner's insights could develop—even more so in the work arising from them—and the general relevance of his contributions could at least become the subject of more open discussion than has thus far been the case. It must be remembered that it was never Steiner's intention to build up an alternative culture; he preferred to influence the course of mainstream culture from within. However, so far, anthroposophical endeavors have not succeeded in this to any major degree, despite the commitment of three generations of students of Anthroposophy, actively working in practical life and professional capacities.

Meanwhile, schools report unprecedented increases in learning difficulties, behavioral problems, and impairment of concentration among pupils; and the general standards of literacy and numeracy seem to be falling for no apparent outer reason. Soil vitality and food quality decrease almost in direct relation to increasing dependency on purely chemical methods of agriculture—the notion that organic alternatives are unaffordable is now beginning to wear thin. Also, in medicine, where technological advances have perhaps come to the most positive expression, a slow degeneration in the general health of the population has to be acknowledged—for example, in the increasing number of immunological disorders, degenerative illnesses, and cancer. In fact, attempts to eliminate the external causes of illness have not contributed to an increase in overall health of the population as had been predicted, although they undoubtedly contributed to an epidemiological shift in the prevalence of acute inflammatory illnesses. Along with technological advances, this shift has always been cited to affirm the success of current forms of medical treatment; even this sign of apparent progress has now been seriously called into question with the publication of reports that allergies and chronic inflammatory conditions are on the increase, particularly among children. Medicine's only solution to this problem, it would seem, is to invest even more in vaccination campaigns—merely reinforcing existing trends—and to increasingly use antibiotics, anti-inflammatory drugs, and chemotherapy. As a long-term solution, medicine now offers terminations of medically undesirable pregnancies and the promise of future possibilities for genetic manipulation.

The emerging "Brave New World" of applied medical reductionism harbors more than its share of unforeseen problems, not to say nightmares. It would be a tragedy if individuals were actually forced to swallow these consequences as though there were no other option. Christopher Fry characterized the modern human condition in his play, *The Sleep of Prisoners*: "Affairs are now soulsize—the enterprise is exploration into God." Very much is at stake, and many battles must still be won before the reductionist Goliath may finally fall from his edifice of supremacy.

In introducing this work to readers of English, I do not profess to any feelings of euphoria. I would nevertheless retain the confidence that it may contribute to reinstating some of the main issues of cognitive science—particularly their implications for the neurosciences—to the place they once occupied in serious scientific study; this could be considered, in its own right, a major breakthrough. The developments that have taken place since Steiner's death, and some of which this introduction has attempted briefly to outline, offer considerable sources of hope that the tide may be turning, as the causes of the downward trends in ecology, education, agriculture, and medicine begin to be diagnosed.

In *Anthroposophy (A Fragment)* we see a remarkable juxtaposition of apparent simplicity of imagery and considerable complexity of thought. To penetrate its content demands strength and discipline on the one hand and, on the other, a childlike naïveté. Even to begin to comprehend the work requires that these faculties have, to some extent, already been trained and integrated. The activity of reading this work will, itself, further enhance these faculties. In the absence of the faculties of discipline and openness, the work will certainly appear totally unintelligible. It challenges both the analytical and inductive aspects of cognition to a degree almost unprecedented, even in Steiner's own writings; this synthesis still has a very unusual ring, even for those of us who may profess to be its advocates. Nevertheless, despite the considerable challenges presented by this work, coupled with inherent linguistic problems—inevitably compounded by translation from the German—it is my conviction that sooner or later it will be acknowledged as having pioneered a way forward, for the neurosciences, in general, and their expressions in professional practice, in particular.

In conclusion, it should be mentioned that Steiner also addressed the subject of the senses and life processes in numerous lectures, primarily from 1909 on, and reference to these will further elaborate and clarify the subject matter covered in *Anthroposophy (A Fragment)*. Hopefully, it will also become clear that the full value and significance of this work can only be rightly assessed in the wider context of Steiner's other written works, some of which have already been mentioned.

In wishing such an unusual work an exciting and fruitful voyage as it enters the seas of the English speaking world, I would commend it into the hands of the guarding spirits of powerlessness, so beautifully evoked in Prospero's words from the Epilogue to Shakespeare's *The Tempest*:

> Gentle breath of yours, my sails
> must fill, or else my project fails,
> which was to please. Now I want
> spirits to enforce, art to enchant;
> and my ending is despair
> unless I be relieved by prayer,
> which pierces so that it assaults
> mercy itself, and frees all faults.
> As you from crimes would pardoned be,
> let your indulgence set me free.

DR. JAMES A. DYSON
Park Attwood Clinic
Stourbridge, UK
February 1995

NOTES

[1] Trust for Cultural Research, Monograph Series No. 22, 1986 (obtainable P.O. Box 13, Tunbridge Wells, Kent, TN3 OJD). A new, much expanded edition of Bortoft's work will be published as *The Wholeness of Nature,* Lindisfarne Press, Hudson, NY, 1996.

[2] See Bertha Mueller (trans.), *Goethe's Botanical Writings,* Ox Bow, 1989, or Douglas Miller (trans.) *Goethe's Scientific Writings,* Princeton University Press, forthcoming.

[3] Available as *Goethean Science*, Mercury Press, Spring Valley, NY.1988. See also John Barnes, *Nature's Open Secret: Rudolf Steiner and Goethe's Participatory Approach to Science*, Anthroposophic Press, Hudson, NY, 1996.

[4] Available as *A Science of Knowing,* Mercury Press, Spring Valley, NY, 1988.

[5] Previously titled *The Philosophy of Freedom* or *The Philosophy of Spiritual Activity*; the new edition is *Intuitive Thinking as a Spiritual Path: A Philosophy of Freedom*, Anthroposophic Press, Hudson, NY, 1995.

[6] Published as *Truth and Knowledge,* Steinerbooks, Blauvelt, NY, 1981. Also titled *Truth and Science*.

[7] See especially *An Outline of Occult Science,* and *Theosophy,* Anthroposophic Press, Hudson, NY.

[8] Philip Laird Johnson's book *The Computer and the Mind* (Fontana, 1988) has been cited as providing the most convincing account to date of this theory.

[9] J. B Watson (1878-1958) was the author among others of *Animal Education* (1903), *Behavior* (1914), *Behaviorism* (1925); I. P. Pavlov (1849-1936) was the author of *Conditioned Reflexes: An Investigation of the Physiological Activity of the Cerebral Cortex*, (Dover Books); B. F. Skinner is

well known for books such as *Beyond Freedom and Dignity* (1971), *About Behaviorism,* and *Walden Two* (1976).

10 See Wolfgang Kohler, *The Task of Gestalt Psychology, Selected Papers, Dynamics in Psychology,* and *The Mentality of Apes*; Max Wertheimer, *Productive Thinking*; Kurt Koffka, *The Growth of the Mind*; Fritz Perls, *The Gestalt Approach & Eyewitness to Therapy* and *Don't Push the River.*

11 Penguin Books. See also *Psychosynthesis* (Penguin).

12 M. Scott Peck, *The Road Less Traveled: A New Psychology of Love, Traditional Values & Spiritual Growth*; and *People of the Lie: The Hope for Healing Human Evil.* Touchstone Books, 1985.

13 Rollo May, *Love and Will,* W. W. Norton & Co., NY, 1969.

14 For Jung's own story of his development, see his book *Memories, Dreams and Reflections.* For Viktor Frankl, the best introduction is his books *The Doctor and the Soul: from Psychotherapy to Logotherapy, Man's Search for Meaning,* and *The Will to Meaning.*

15 Gerald M. Edelman, *Bright Air, Brilliant Fire: On the Matter of the Mind,* Basic Books, 1993. See also *Neural Darwinism: The Theory of Neuronal Group Selection* (1987) and *The Remembered Present: A Biological Theory of Consciousness* (1989).

16 See Owen Barfield (ed./trans.), *The Case for Anthroposophy,* Rudolf Steiner Press, London, 1970.

Robert Sardello

This remarkable work by Rudolf Steiner concerns the human senses, the life processes, and the forming of the human body; and it provides a basis for an anthroposophical understanding of the human being. It is also an indispensable foundation for the development of a spiritual psychology that adheres to an anthroposophical mode of thought. Rudolf Steiner himself indicated that the study of the human soul follows from an examination of the senses, and from there it is necessary to move to a study of the human spirit. These three areas constitute Anthroposophy in a restricted sense—for the field encompasses much more—and all that is needed to form spiritual psychology can be found in them.

Knowledge gained by careful observation alone is the basis for research in a spiritual psychology founded on an understanding of the human being as a revelation of the spiritual worlds. It does not require crossing into spiritual worlds with clairvoyance, though it benefits greatly from the observations of those who have developed such capacities. Such a psychology does require a heightening of observational capacities to correctly understand what can be known about the human soul through observation alone, and the only provision is that the observer be included in what is observed. One must become aware of the act of cognizing as an essential part of what is known. Spiritual psychology needs to develop to the very edges of observational capacities, where the presence of the spiritual worlds can be detected. But, spiritual psychology always reaches toward those worlds, while not crossing over into them. The other side of spiritual psychology is concerned with how soul enters every moment into physical life, and this makes it necessary to have a living understanding of the senses and the life processes. This aspect of the foundation of spiritual psychology is the subject of *Anthroposophy (A Fragment)*.

In this work, we not only learn about the human senses and life processes in an entirely different way than through physiology and contemporary sensory psychology, but we also learn how to actively meditate on these processes. New capacities of observation can thus be formed. The intensely compact character of the writing presents itself hieroglyphically. The aim is not to interpret what is said, but to enter into it, to simultaneously enter into the activity of the senses and life processes themselves. By entering into this text meditatively we are not only being informed, but also being formed into beings who can make observations within the activity of what we are observing. It is as though the senses and life processes themselves are doing the speaking. What better training could there be for developing the style of thinking needed for accurate and descriptive presence to the mobile activity of soul and spirit life? If observations concerning our sensory life are handled as if sensing were a mechanical process, subject to description in terms of causes and effects, it is certain that our understanding of soul and spirit life would be falsely portrayed. The inner life would either be taken up and spoken of in the language of cause and effect, or it would be presented as a confusion of mystical, sentimental and religious speculation passing as science. Thus, a study of this work can be a source of extreme discomfort, as if losing one's mooring in the world of fixity. However, staying with this discomfort will gradually open up the world in entirely new ways and prepare us for even more mobile considerations as steps are taken into the inner life.

Those familiar with Anthroposophy have probably encountered Steiner's enumeration of twelve senses rather than the usual five to eight described by sensory physiology. In this text, however, only ten senses are described; both the sense for the I of another—the capacity to actually sense something of the true individuality of another person—and the sense of touch are not considered here to be senses in their own right.

In the last appendix, however, the capacity of the I to experience another, separate I while listening empathetically to what manifests through the tone of another human being is described as the archetype of an organ of perception.

To ordinary experience, touch undoubtedly seems to be a sense, the cause of which sensory physiology attributes to nerve endings at the surface of the skin. According to Steiner, the experience of touch can be accounted for solely by the combined effects of the sense of life, the sense of self-movement, and the sense of balance. What we call an experience of the sense of touch is actually a judgment based upon the immediate experience of these other three senses. The sense of touch, conveying nothing but "pure otherness," is devoid of sense experience in its own right.

The I-experience and the sense of touch form the two boundaries of the realm of sense experience.

The enumeration of the senses and what they do is quite revealing, but they are so clearly presented by Steiner that comment here is unnecessary. More revealing and significant for spiritual psychology is how different clusters of senses operate in relation to each other to bring about definite experiences.

The life sense, the sense of self-movement, and the sense of balance operate together to give us awareness of ourselves as physical beings. We know we are physical beings because this is first felt internally. The feeling of bodilyness is the soul's perception of the external world that comes nearest to the soul. This observation is important because the combined activity of these three senses then also provide the border, going the other way, into soul life proper. These three senses comprise a sort of boundary condition between soul life and external physical existence, which for the soul is the experience of an inner bodily state. For example, when we feel "out of sorts"—fatigued, stressed, ill, and so on—such states are experienced due to the life sense. But, at the same time, these states touch upon purely psychological qualities. In such a state we also feel out of balance, which is truly related to the sense of balance, and we also feel acutely uncomfortable with our physical position in the world, which is related to the sense of self-movement. Due to the combined qualities of these three senses and their closeness to soul life, such psychological states of discomfort have a distinctly bodily character to them and can only be described as an overall condition without much specificity. Therefore, it can be suggested that these states are likely to improve by giving attention to conditions of bodily health. On the other hand, if there is not an awareness of this boundary between these senses and soul life, and complaints are handled as if they were solely psychological, it is quite possible that imbalance will be driven into the soul. Spiritual psychology would thus be very interested in investigating the subtleties of these senses.

The senses of smell, taste, sight, warmth, and hearing form a kind of progression in which we are taken increasingly into not just the physical world, but even into the interior of physical things. We not only sense what is "out there," we also sense what is inside what is "out there." Through these senses, then, we can actually apprehend something of the soul of the world. The visual appearance of a thing in its color, for example, not only reveals its outer aspect, but already expresses something of its inner nature. Speaking in the second chapter about hearing, Steiner stated: "It is more than merely metaphorical to say that a body's soul comes to manifestation through sound." A reflection such as this, if taken up in the forming of a spiritual psychology, vastly increases the range of the usual concerns of psychology. We need a psychology of the outer world in order to balance the possibilities of self-absorption and egotism, which are bound to occur when care of the soul is taken only to mean one's own soul, as if the outer world was not also included in the sphere of soul life.

The speech, or tone, sense is not concerned with understanding the meaning of what another person says, but rather with the immediate bodily sensation caused by phonetic tones, and through this sense we gain the ability to recognize the tremendously important difference between soul located in the world of physical things and the human soul. We discover through the speech sense that the soul of a body is alive, and further, that the soul reveals itself as freed from the bodily aspect. We speak by means of the body, but speech itself can be sensed as free of the body. Sensing speech not only involves sounds, but also gestures and facial expressions, which also utilize the body, yet go beyond it. The speech sense is so important because it verifies the existence of human soul life. Soul is not a matter of speculation, nor is it at first a matter of religious sentiment or metaphysical argument; it is directly sensed, preceding any thinking or judgment. It can be suggested, therefore, that any attempts to work with the soul life of another, such as in psychotherapy, would do well indeed to concentrate on a training oriented toward the speech sense. This would avoid falsely attributing qualities to the soul that actually arise from thinking and judgment rather than from actual observation. Here, we might point to the extremely valuable work of current psychoanalysts, such as W. R. Bion and especially Christopher Bollas, who have developed a highly sophisticated inner discipline of deliberately forgetting what occurs with a patient from session to session, in order to be present in the mode of sensation. These analysts pay particular attention to the whole sensory array within which a session takes place, not seeking to analyze it, but sensing the immediate soul qualities unfolding before their eyes. In particular, they give attention to the speech of the patient, rather than to the meaning of what is spoken.

The same is true of what Steiner describes as the sense of concept. This sense does not reveal the meaning of what another person is thinking but is a direct apprehension of the activity of thinking of another person. Sensitive observation through this sense is imperative for soul work and involves learning to pay attention to the fact that we understand immediately, without judgment or evaluation. Therapeutic psychology has always taken the stance that another person must be understood without judgment. Usually, however, this stance is taken in a negative sense—stay away from judging. For the most part, what has actually come about in therapeutic psychology is that one should understand whatever is heard in a positive light, which is no less a judgment. Instead, approaching the soul life of another person should mean developing the capacity to be more present to another person through the sense of concept.

An essential and most important difference between an anthroposophically based spiritual psychology and the only other specifically soul-oriented psychology—the analytical psychology of C. G. Jung—can be found in the third chapter of *Anthroposophy (A Fragment)*. While Steiner does not mention Jung, it is important to mention Jung at this point, because analytic psychology lacks an appreciation for the sensory basis of soul life.[1] On the other hand, Steiner recognized that the dynamics of soul life—desire, sympathy, antipathy, urges, wishes, willing—stem from the way in which sensing is taken up by the soul. Jung and Steiner do wholeheartedly agree, however, that soul life itself is constituted by the activity of images. For Jung, the ultimate source of soul images is the archetypes, and that is the way he accounted for the very organization of soul life. Steiner saw that the organization of soul life is not due to archetypes, but rather to what we each call our own *I*. At the beginning of the third chapter Steiner says, "A sensory perception becomes a soul experience when it is taken up out of the senses' domain and into the realm of the I." In Jung's psychology, the I is at first a complex of the soul, before conscious work toward individuation takes place. This means that our ego—the ordinary sense of the I—is but a small part of soul life with which we identify, and takes itself to be all there is. Through the individuation process, the ego sense of the I enlarges into the experience of the Self, which bears some resemblance to the I as described by Steiner.

---

1. Rudolf Steiner addressed the problems of analytical psychology and the need for a spiritual psychology in five lectures collected under the title *Psychoanalysis & Spiritual Psychology*, Anthroposophic Press, Hudson, NY, 1990.

Steiner, out of his careful observation connected with the world, saw that the I is actually more comprehensive than the soul. We could say that the soul exists within the I, which is the exact reverse of Jung's view. As interest in a spiritual psychology grows within Anthroposophy, it is apparent that this difference is not often fully appreciated. Currently, numerous writings in Anthroposophy speak quite loosely about archetypes, and do not sufficiently distinguish between their use of archetypes and the way they were spoken of by Jung. Once the difference is established, a truly meaningful dialogue can be established between Jung's psychology and spiritual psychology, one which can prove to be most fruitful. For example, archetypes do not change for Jung, but are permanent patterns, experienced within the soul as archetypal images—such as the wise old man, the mother, or the divine child archetype. Anthroposophy recognizes that the I, the very center of soul life, does change due to life experiences and that archetypal images evolve and change with the evolution of consciousness. The current popularization of Jung's psychology perpetuates an atavistic belief that the way to soul experience is through obliterating the ego. Even Jung did not hold this view, but such a misunderstanding shows the great need for a phenomenology of the I. The I—such a small and overly commonplace word—is in fact tremendously complex. The I cannot be understood without moving toward it through an investigation of the senses.

Steiner followed the description of the senses with an investigation into the origin of the senses. Again, from chapter three, here is a sentence requiring much meditation: "Before the world can present itself to human beings as sense perception, the senses themselves must be born out of it." Because we ordinarily take ourselves, in our bodily existence, to be simply inserted into the world which spreads before our senses, we are not able to see the *almost* seamless mobile connection between sensing and what is sensed, and we do not consider what must be behind what is sensed. A whole different kind of thinking is required to bring this to reflection. At this point in Steiner's text, the mode of reflection has moved to a different level, and this is where you can begin to feel like you are swimming without any land in sight. At the same time, it would be a grave mistake to think that Steiner has become abstract; it is quite the opposite case. Our usual way of thinking is highly abstract, and thus when confronted with a careful description of experience from within the experience itself, a major adjustment of consciousness is required.

The world that forms the senses—senses which in turn give us access to the world from which they were formed, now in a physical manner—is a world beyond perception, a supersensible world. How do we know this? If there were not a world of warmth beyond the senses and beyond the physical world, it would not be possible for there to be organs for the perception of warmth. If there were not a world of sound, the organs would not be possible for the sensing of sound; and so it is for all the senses. Is Steiner speaking here of the embryological development of the senses, or the act of sensing as it occurs each moment? Both. More can be said of this supersensible world. It is at one and the same time varied and unified. The world beyond the senses forms the sense organs as well as what is sensed by the sense organs, and is as varied as the number of senses. But, insofar as we are able to say "I see a tree," "I hear a bell," and "I experience the world immediately without the intervention of thought," we are also able to say that the supersensible world is unified as the I is unified.

The I is not a subjective or merely personal experience; it is the whole, unified supersensible world condensed to a point, experienced now from within. Neither the I, nor the supersensible world, which is necessary for there to be a sense world and senses, belong to sensory life as such. Furthermore, we are not merely physical bodies with various sense organs inserted at various points, unrelated to the body as a whole. Certain of the senses—life, self-movement, balance—work also as forces from within the whole body, while shaping individual sense organs in accordance with the wholeness of the body. Other senses—smell, taste, sight, warmth, hearing—work as forces that meet these inner forces and shape sense organs at the surface of the body. With the sense of tone (or word), and the sense of concept, the direction of the supersensible forces that form sense organs is wholly from without. Having pointed to these facts, we can now say something more about the nature of the I: The I is the inner expression of the supersensible forces forming the sense world and the sense organs.

The I was referred to above as a point-like condensation within of the supersensible world that forms the sense organs and the world to be sensed. This description, while accurate, might convey an impression of the I as static. However, it is far from static. In chapter 6 we are given a marvelous phenomenology of the I in relation to sensing. For example, the I functions in relation to the sense of smell by sending out its own being toward the world, but not quite reaching an outer object. Instead, the outer object sends its own being toward the body, and the I is thrown back before it meets the object, as if the outer world invades the I. This activity constitutes smell. Steiner's descriptions of the activities of the I in relation to each of the senses are truly magnificent and worthy of contemplation. We can conclude from such contemplation that the I is not static and, in fact, constantly undergoes changes due to its encounters with sense experiences. And, if this is so, then a further conclusion follows: If the I changes, then the supersensible world—which is the I expanded out to a world beyond the senses—also changes due to individual experiences of the world.

Notice where we have come to in this rather complex exposition. We have gone from a simple, everyday notion of the senses to an understanding of how the body is formed. We have also come to the point of having to say that there must indeed be a spiritual world, but solely on the basis of observing what can be known through description alone. No theory is involved, and clairvoyant perception is not relied upon. Further, we have moved into a dynamic mode of thinking in which the act of thinking, and what is thought about, play against each other like waves in relation to the ocean. We have also come to see the I as basic to the formation of a spiritual psychology. The validity of the term, *spiritual psychology*, also becomes apparent. The I is a purely spiritual experience, a condensation within of the supersensible world. Soul experiences occur within the I. A psychology that fully recognizes the reflection of the supersensible, spiritual world within, and is concerned with the soul—as the word, *psychology*, or logos of the soul, implies—is rightly named spiritual psychology. Let us now turn to the life processes and their relation to the senses.

Steiner describes seven life processes: breathing, warming, nourishing, secreting, maintaining, growing, and generating. All of these processes are described as we actually experience them in bodily life. A wonderful exercise consists of meditation on these descriptions as a way of coming to a healthy connection with our body. Such exercises are also of vital importance for developing spiritual psychology; a picture can be built up showing the configuring of the human body from the inside out and taking place through these processes. More importantly, we can see the intimate link between the forming of the human body from within through these life processes, and the emotional experiences as the sense organs are linked to the I.

Emotional experience is usually felt as a disturbance in one or more of the life processes. For example, a disturbance in breathing is felt as anxiety; a disturbance of nourishing is felt as an uncomfortable gnawing within, and the judgment of such gnawing is experienced as hunger. When the life processes are balanced, an emotional well-being is felt. Note that the I does not penetrate the life processes. Thus, what we often speak of as emotional experiences are actually judgments made concerning emotional life. For example, to say "I feel anxious," is not an emotional experience but a conclusion arrived at through thinking about what one directly feels, but we do not have this clarity of consciousness within the emotion itself. Emotional experiences do not need the I to conclude that they are happening. The conclusion is revealed instinctively.

The life processes and their accompanying emotional states cannot be lumped together as if they were the same thing. On the other hand, the kind of thinking Steiner engaged in did not conceive of the life processes as belonging only to physiology and the emotions as belonging only in the domain of psychological experience. Since there is a supersensible world that forms the sense organs and the sense world—revealed within the person as the I—so there must also be a world that forms the organs of the life processes, as well as what is experienced through the life processes, as an ongoing emotional life. The world that forms the organs of the life processes, Steiner called *the world of life*; and the inner point of this world of life that instinctively reveals an experience of the life processes, he called the *astral human being*. The organs of the life processes include the lungs, the heart, the circulation of the blood—and probably the other major organs of the body, such as the liver and the kidneys, though here they are not named. The organs of the life processes approach a flowing into one another; they are not as separate as the sense organs. Thus, different kinds of emotional experiences are easily confused with one another, and we also experience this directly—it is possible to be flooded with emotion and not be clear whether an emotional experience such as anxiety is related to breathing alone, or is perhaps centered more in another organ, which it turn affects breathing. Emotional life is far more mobile than sensory life, and this tells us that the *life world* must be imagined quite differently than the higher spiritual world, which forms the sense organs. The life world can be imagined as one in which different currents do not interpenetrate, but run into each other—or as Steiner puts it, overrun each other.

In addition to the instinctive experiences of the life processes mentioned above, there are feeling-like experiences which do not occur as a result of the life processes. These experiences are also not activities of the I. Three such experiences are: impulses to movement that are apparently free of the life processes; desires; and *images* that arise from sensory experience. These experiences are not connected with particular bodily organs, but rather to organs of the astral human being. Of particular importance for psychological reflection is the relationship between images and desires.

Sensory experience lasts only as long as a sense organ is focused on an object, but we can turn away from the object and hold it in an inner way. What remains after the sense experience is an experience of the astral being. Images do not involve sensory organs or the organs of the life processes. The organs involved with images are not sense-perceptible but are the organs of the astral body. Images can penetrate the force of desire and, becoming desires, live on in movement. Images arise first, then desires, which finally become movement. Thus, we have a sensory experience which lives on as an image, the image lives on as desire, and desire lives on as movement. Impulses, desires, and sensory images thus do not belong to sensory life directly, nor can they properly be called soul experiences. Current psychology lacks an understanding of the astral realm and thus wrongly interprets these experiences as physiological conditions or as psychological experiences.

Let us further compare the anthroposophical understanding of emotional experience with what is typically offered by current psychology. First, current psychology has no way to relate organ processes to emotions other than in terms of cause and effect. It is, of course, well established in psychology that organ states are somehow related to emotions, but the connection is most often made by way of the brain. For example, a recent medical study reported that emotional support of heart attack victims by those close to them resulted in a significantly increased rate of recovery. The researchers reported that emotional support resulted in increased levels of norepinephrine and cortisol in the brain. The study further said that the exact role of those chemicals on the heart is unclear, but that they are believed to affect blood pressure and the heart's response to stress. The organs are taken to be no more than physiological processes, and emotions are described without reference to the body in a specific way. Psychologists who work with emotional life fare no better, and simply say that emotional stress can be physically debilitating.

There are many complex theories concerning emotions, both ancient and modern, but complexity does not necessarily constitute an adequate explanation. These theories almost always seek to coordinate physiological, chemical, neurological, visceral, sensorial, and the conscious and unconscious processes. All of the pieces are there, but they never result in a truly comprehensive view such as Steiner offered. By far the best investigation of emotions within current psychology is James Hillman's work.[2] After a thorough consideration of existent theories, he came to see the therapeutic significance of emotion in terms of the development of courage to face the emotions consciously. To be able to face emotion in this way, he proposed that the concept of *psyche* must be returned to psychology. Psyche has long been abandoned in favor of cognitive process, behavior, neurology, physiology, and so on. He pointed out that we cannot face emotion from the viewpoint of ego consciousness, from which it always escapes. Hillman uses the word *psyche* to mean an organizing function that brings together the outer and inner worlds, and *emotion* is the energetic activity of the psyche. However, by establishing the psyche as a viewpoint, the specificity of bodily processes begins to disappear and is replaced by

---

2. James Hillman, *Emotion: A Comprehensive Phenomenology of Theories and their Meanings for Therapy*, Routledge & Kegan Paul, London, 1960.

images that do not arise from observation of emotional phenomena themselves, but are imported from myths, art, and literature as a means of amplifying and clarifying emotional life. For example, he utilizes the image of a charioteer and his horses as an image of the way in which we are driven by emotional life—how we are connected to emotions by means of the reins, with which we drive the horses, and yet, are also being driven by them.

Modern psychology either tries to reduce emotional experience to physiological and neural processes, or it creates a concept of parallelism between physiology and psychological states, linking them together causally. Or it may depart altogether from the specificity of bodily life as essential to emotion. Modern psychology does not have the tools to give an adequate account of emotional life; its concepts are either too small or too general. Rudolf Steiner shows us that emotional experiences are neither just physiological processes, nor soul experiences alone—nor a combination of these. Psychology needs the concept of the *life world*, which forms the organs of the life processes. And, psychology needs the concept of the *astral human being*—to begin with, the inner reflection of the life world—which is necessary for an understanding of how emotions are lived through the inner life organs of the body, but are, at the same time, experiences almost beyond the body. Finally, psychology needs an imagination of the astral human being, the being that has organs for experiencing impulses, desires, and sensory images. These concepts are not inserted as a theory, but can be seen as facts through careful observation.

The final chapters of *Anthroposophy (A Fragment)*— beginning with chapter seven—are extremely complex, and Steiner was not satisfied with them. He pointed out that he did not have adequate language to express ideas in writing as he could in lectures, where he formed pictures through repetition and emphasis. Nonetheless, these chapters are well worth struggling with.

Before the close of the nineteenth century, Rudolf Steiner wrote in the section on the primal phenomenon in chapter sixteen of *Goethean Science*:[3] "The picture of the world presented to the senses is the sum of metamorphosing contents of perception, without matter underlying it." This theme was worked out by Steiner in these later chapters. Substance is imagined here, not as consisting of atoms and molecules, but as imaginations formed out of the different sense experiences themselves. Different "inversions" of sense organs play a key role. Underlying the sense organs and life organs are different worlds that interplay in various ways, from which both space itself and the human form unfolds.

These latter chapters are of particular importance to spiritual psychology for several reasons. Developing an imagination of the forming of the various organs, life organs, and the form of the human body can result in a new spiritual psychology of development. Research is needed that relates what Steiner has written here and what psychology usually presents as developmental phases.

---

3. *Goethean Science*, Mercury Press, Spring Valley, NY, 1988. (The above quote was retranslated.)

Some of this work has been done by Bernard Lievegoed from an anthroposophical point of view, but it is only a beginning.[4] It is also possible to imagine new approaches to cognitive and language development, approaches that explicitly take into account the human being as a revelation of the spiritual worlds.[5] But, more basically, these chapters form the foundation for meditative work that can result in doing the work of psychology with a living imagination of the human being. Psychology does not currently have such an imagination and is particularly deficient in understanding the living body. Its concepts of the body come wholly from biology and physiology; and, consequently, the mode of thinking in psychology is divided between causal thinking dependent on empirical natural scientific concepts that natural science itself has outgrown, as well as imagistic and mythological modes of thought that ignore the human body altogether.

These last chapters also impress upon us the conclusion that spiritual psychology needs to be a completely new psychology. We do not yet have such a psychology. It is a new field. Pieces taken from other psychologies here and there—parts that seem compatible with anthroposophy—will only produce untold confusion without a clear understanding of the human being as a revelation of the spiritual worlds. This view provides the basis for evaluating what

---

4. Bernard Lievegoed, *Phases: The Spiritual Rhythms of Adult Life*, Rudolf Steiner Press, Bristol, UK, 1993.

5. Linda Sussman, *Speech of the Grail: A Journey toward Speaking that Heals and Transforms*, Lindisfarne Press, Hudson, NY, 1995.

is of importance from other psychologies and what we need to leave behind. The possibilities of a fruitful, therapeutic psychology based on the spiritual psychology imagined here is even further away. In this work by Steiner, we can see that it will require meditative training that starts with extended concentration on bodily life as spirit-revelation. It will then need to incorporate a second level of meditative training that focuses on what can be known of the human soul by observation alone. Finally, a third level of meditation will be required, focusing on the edges of soul life, where it meets with spirit life. Only on such foundation will it then be possible to begin developing a therapeutic, spiritual psychology. It is my hope that this work by Steiner becomes a sort of handbook for the first phase of this work.

ROBERT SARDELLO
School of Spiritual Psychology
Great Barrington, Massachusetts

Rudolf Steiner's usage of words is the opposite of cementing meanings. The actual words often leave considerable leeway for possible meaning, sometimes annoyingly so. This is due in part to the nature of the German language. In English this flexibility is frequently impossible, or simply leads to an insipid style. The English language generally renders more precisely and colorfully than the German by its very necessity of choice—there are many more words to choose from in English than in German. However, their shades of meaning often have a narrower range, which essentially leaves no other choice than to be more precise through the choice of words than in the original German.

On the one hand, this can make such translations difficult, particularly with a book like *Anthroposophy*, which remained a fragment—according to Steiner himself—because the very language did not yet allow him to coin the necessary modalities of expression. This, I believe, is not a problem of the German language in particular, but of current modern language in general. Language itself must evolve to accommodate the thoughts of something like an anthroposophy. History shows that this is not unreasonable at all: language has been anything but static over the centuries, and this becomes apparent, for example, in the fact that a large number of current common expressions in German were actually coined in the poetry of Goethe (in English, the prime example, of course, is Shakespeare).

On the other hand, I do concur with Michael Lipson in believing that a translation can actually become clearer than the original.[1] At the risk of seeming immodest, I do think that, in a few instances, this has been achieved.

DETLEF HARDORP
Falkensee, Germany

---

1. See the Translator's Introduction in *Intuitive Thinking as a Spiritual Path: A Philosophy of Freedom,* which is a new translation by Michael Lipson for the centennial edition of *The Philosophy of Spiritual Activity.*

Anthroposophy, an incomplete work dating from 1910, was found among Rudolf Steiner's unpublished works both in the form of a handwritten manuscript and as printed sheets corrected by the author. Rudolf Steiner had dealt with the same theme orally in the first two of his twelve lectures on "Anthroposophy, Psychosophy, and Pneumatosophy," given in Berlin in 1909, 1910, and 1911,[1] and later returned to it repeatedly from various points of view (see appendix beginning on page 171). The content of this fragment is so valuable that its publication seems justified, even though the work remained unfinished and was never published by Rudolf Steiner himself.

Rudolf Steiner's thoughts about these pages and how they are meant to be taken are evident from discussions of the same content in passages from two lectures, the seventh lecture in the cycle *The Boundaries of Natural Science* (October 2, 1920)[2] and the sixth lecture in the cycle

---

1. *The Wisdom of Man, of the Soul, and of the Spirit*, Anthroposophic Press, Spring Valley, 1971. (GA 115, to be republished 1996.)
2. *The Boundaries of Natural Science,* Anthroposophic Press, Spring Valley, NY, 1983.

Anthroposophy and Science (given six months later, on March 22, 1921).[3]

On October 2, 1920, in Dornach, Rudolf Steiner said:

Many years ago, in a specific domain [of spiritual-scientific research], I attempted to find the words to clothe what can be called a theory of the human senses. I succeeded, after a fashion, in finding words to present this theory of the twelve senses in oral lectures, because speaking allows more possibility to maneuver language and use repetition to ensure understanding. In this way, the shortcomings of our language, which is not yet capable of expressing a supersensible essence like this, are not so keenly felt. As I said, this was many years ago. When I then attempted to write down in book form what I had presented orally in lectures as the real anthroposophy, something very strange happened. In the process of bearing inward what had been experienced outwardly, it become something so sensitive that language would not relinquish the words. I think the first section of several sixteen-page sheets lay at the printer's for five or six years. I wanted to continue in the same style as the beginning, but I could not go on writing, simply because the language would not relinquish what I wanted to achieve to someone at my stage of development. After that, I was overburdened

---

3. *Anthroposophy and Science: Observation, Experiment, Mathematics,* Mercury Press, Spring Valley, NY, 1991.

with work and, to this day, I have been unable to finish the book. Those less conscientious in how they
handle what they receive from the spiritual world and
then pass it on to their fellow human beings may
smile at how I came to a halt in the face of an obstacle
that was insurmountable at the time. But others, those
who have truly experienced and are capable of taking
full responsibility for the results when they depict the
paths to Imagination that humanity in the West must
follow, know that many things are needed to find the
right words for this depiction. As a path of development, this is relatively easy to portray, as has been
done in my book *How to Know Higher Worlds*.[4] But,
in aiming at very specific results, such as describing
the essential nature of the human senses—part of the
inner organization of the human being—it becomes
difficult to grasp the Imaginations and to use words
to represent them in sharp outline.[5]

And in Stuttgart on March 22, 1921:

I once lectured to the Theosophical Society on what
I called "anthroposophy," presenting as much about
it as my spiritual research had yielded. I was asked
to have these lectures printed, and I proceeded to
write these things down, but in writing them down,

---

4. *How to Know Higher Worlds: A Modern Path of Initiation,*
Anthroposophic Press, Hudson, NY, 1994.
5. Cf. *The Boundaries of Natural Science*, 102.

they turned into something different. Not that any part of the original was changed, but it became necessary to add certain things by way of further explanation. It also became necessary to formulate these things more precisely. That took one year, and then a new opportunity arose—the Society's General Assembly was taking place again. People wanted to have the "anthroposophical" lectures for sale at the General Assembly, so they would have to be finished. I then announced a new and different lecture cycle for the coming meeting; I sent the first sheets of *Anthroposophy* off to the printer and they were promptly printed. I thought I would be able to go on writing, and did indeed continue for a while, but it became ever more necessary to supplement the more detailed explanations. In the end, a number of sheets were printed, as much as I had written, but one sheet had only thirteen or fourteen of its sixteen pages full. The rest were blank, and I was supposed to go on writing. Meanwhile—there were also other reasons for the whole thing, other things contributing to the end result, but I want to tell you the one reason that has to do with what we are discussing here—the point came where I said to myself, "Finishing this thing the way I really want it to be, the way it really ought to be, now that a year has gone by, requires developing in detail a specific conceptual method, a specific adaptation of imaginative, inspired knowledge, and applying this method of arriving at knowledge to these anthroposophical questions." My next step was negative—I simply dropped *Anthroposophy*. I intended to do the research needed to continue it, but today it is still as it was then, with many sheets already printed. However, I then became closely acquainted with something I now want to describe to you, although I can only do so schematically. It consists of a great number of inner experiences that are actually research methods, methods of arriving at knowledge of the human being.

It became ever more apparent that a complete formulation of "anthroposophy," as it was then intended, was possible only under the following conditions. In our inner vision, we must be able to see how to extend what we see working as spiritual and soul activity in our nervous system when we observe with real inner sight, how to extend it until we arrive at a certain point where we clearly notice that all of the spiritual and soul activity that proceeds from outside inward and that we grasp in the act of Imagination and Inspiration, *all this is crossing itself.* (The point is actually a line standing vertically, but I am only going to present it schematically here—with regard to certain phenomena the point is further up or further down, but to depict it all in detail may not be possible in these lectures, so I will simply present a cross section of the whole thing, as it were.) Because it is crossing, however, we are no longer free in practicing this activity. Not that we were totally free before, as I described, but now we become even less free. We notice that the whole thing is undergoing a change. We are entering a state of being more strongly held in our imaginative and inspired visualization. Speaking concretely, if we use imaginative and inspired visualization to grasp what sense perception and its rational extension are for the eye—that is, if we manage to grasp the organ of sight by means of Imagination permeated with Inspiration—this activity extends inward and a crossing takes place. Then, with the activity with which we first embraced the eye, we embrace a different organ. Essentially, it is the kidney.

The same thing happens with other organs. When we extend this imaginative and inspired activity into the inner human being, we always find that what we grasp with it is an organ that is already complete, at least in its potentials, when a person is born. Thus we advance to a real inner perception of the human organism. This presents a very specific difficulty and, since at that time I was supposed not only to finish the book but also to give a different lecture cycle that also required research, you can imagine that it was not easy to cope with this method in that stage of its development, many years ago.

In addition, I must mention the difficulty of initially being repeatedly pushed back. The actual ability to continue is something that requires holding on to your inner strength if you are to succeed. Again and again you must undertake to strengthen and intensify your power of conceptualization, the inner work you do in your soul to love outer nature. Otherwise, you will simply be easily repulsed each time. You notice that you are going inward, into yourself, but you are always pushed back out again and, instead of receiving what I want to call "inner vision," you get something that is not correct. This being pushed back is a development that must be overcome.

I wanted to tell you this story so that you see that a spiritual researcher can actually point to the moments where specific problems of spiritual research are wrestled with. Unfortunately, in the years following the event I have described, and especially in the last few years, my time has been so filled with every conceivable thing that finishing *Anthroposophy*—something I consider a particularly necessary and even indispensable activity—could not take place.[6]

The text reproduced here follows the proofs through page 165. The rest has been taken from the manuscript. In places the proofs include alternate versions, which are printed here at the end of some chapters.

Of the additions that have been included (Appendices 1–5), the first three are from recently discovered manuscript pages that represent modifications of the text as it is reproduced here. They were not included by Rudolf Steiner because they did not fit into the framework of the rest of the content. Appendix 4, a draft for a final text, was included in the 1951 edition. Appendix 5 is a separate treatment of a related topic.

---

6. Cf. *Anthroposophy and Science*, 107–110.

CHAPTER 1

THE CHARACTER
OF ANTHROPOSOPHY

Since ancient times, studying the human being has been felt to be the worthiest branch of human research. Yet, if we allow ourselves to be affected by all that is known about human beings—all the knowledge that has come to light throughout the ages—it is easy to become discouraged. Our questions about what a human being really is, and what our relationship to the universe is, are answered by a plethora of opinions and, as we ponder these opinions, we realize that they differ in manifold ways. As a result, we may feel that we are not called upon to undertake investigations of this sort and that we must give up hope of ever satisfying our desire to understand.

This feeling would be justified only if perceiving different views of an object were actually evidence that we are incapable of recognizing something true about that object. Those who accept this position would have to believe that no talk of knowledge or understanding is possible unless the complete nature of an object discloses itself to us all at once. But the human way of knowing is not such that the nature of things can be imparted all at once; it is more like painting or photographing a tree from a particular side. The picture gives the full truth of what the tree looks like from a certain point of view, but, if we select a different point of view, the picture becomes quite different. Only the combined effect of a series of pictures from various points of view can give an overall idea of the tree.

But this is the only way we can consider the things and beings of the world. We must necessarily state whatever we are capable of saying about them as views that hold true from different vantage points. This is the case not only with regard to observing things with our senses; it is also true in the spiritual domain—although we must not let ourselves be led astray by this comparison and imagine that differences in points of view in the latter have anything to do with spatial relationships. Every view can be a true view, if it faithfully reproduces what is observed. It is refuted only if it is proved to be legitimately contradicted by another view from *the same perspective*. That it differs with a view from a different perspective generally means nothing. Taking this position safeguards us against the insubstantial objection that in such a case every opinion must necessarily appear justified. When we see the tree from a specified vantage point, our image of the tree must have a particular shape; similarly, a spiritual view from a specified perspective must also have a particular form. It is clear, however, that we can demonstrate an error in a view only if we are clear on its perspective.

If we always kept this in mind, we would fare much better in the world of human opinions than is often the case. We would then realize that in many cases differences of opinion stem only from differences in perspective. Only by means of different but true views can we approach the essence of things. The errors that people make along these lines do not stem from individuals arriving at different views, but result from each person wishing to perceive his or her own view as the only justifiable one.

There is a readily available objection to all this. It could be said that, if we want to represent the truth, we should not merely provide one way of looking at the thing in question but should rather rise above all possible viewpoints to a holistic understanding. This may sound like a reasonable demand. However, it cannot possibly be met. What a thing is *must* be characterized from different points of view. The comparison to a tree that is painted from different perspectives seems relevant here. Someone who refuses to abide by these different views of the tree in arriving at an overall image might paint a very blurry, hazy picture, but there would be no truth in it. Similarly, truth cannot be gained from an understanding that seeks to encompass an object in a single glance, but only from putting together the true views resulting from different perspectives. This may not accommodate human impatience, but it does correspond to the realities we learn to recognize as we cultivate a richer striving for knowledge.

Little can lead us as firmly toward a real appreciation for the truth as such a striving for knowledge. This appreciation is rightly called *real*, because it cannot bring faint-heartedness in its wake. Because it recognizes the truth itself within truth's limitations, this appreciation does not lead us to despair of striving for truth. However, it does safeguard us against empty arrogance that believes that, in its own possession of the truth, it encompasses the full nature of things.

If we take these considerations sufficiently into account, we will find it understandable that we ought to strive for knowledge—especially knowledge of the human being— by attempting to approach the essence of our subject from different points of view. *One* such viewpoint—characterizable as lying midway between two others, as it were— has been chosen for what is being pointed to here. This is not to suggest that there are not many other viewpoints in addition to the three that we will consider. However, these three have been chosen as being especially characteristic.

The first point of view is that of *anthropology*. This science assembles what we can observe about human beings through our senses. Then, from the results of this observation, it attempts to draw conclusions about the essential nature of the human being. For example, it considers how our sense organs work, the shape and structure of our bones, the conditions that prevail in our nervous system, the processes involved when our muscles move, and so forth. Anthropology applies its methods to penetrating into the more subtle structure of our organs in an attempt to recognize the necessary conditions for feeling, conceptualization, and so forth. It also investigates similarities between human beings and animals and attempts to arrive at a concept of how human beings are related to other living things. It continues by investigating the living conditions of aboriginal peoples, who seem to have been left behind in evolution in comparison with the civilized nations. From these observations it develops ideas about what more developed peoples, who have passed the stage of development at which aboriginal peoples have remained, were once like. It investigates the remains of prehistoric human beings in the strata of the earth and formulates concepts about how civilization has progressed. It investigates the influence of climate, the oceans, and other geographical conditions on human life. It tries to gain a perspective on the circumstances surrounding the evolution of the various races and ethnic lifestyles, on rights, the development of writing and languages, and so forth. In this context, we are applying the name "anthropology" to the totality of our physical studies of the human being, including not only what is often attributed to it in the narrower sense of the word, but also human morphology, biology, and so on.

As a rule, anthropology stays within the currently recognized limits of the scientific method. It has accumulated a monumental amount of information, and the ways of thinking applied in summing this up differ considerably. In spite of this, anthropology has a very beneficial contribution to make to our understanding of human nature, and it is constantly adding new information. In accord with our modern way of looking at things, great hopes are placed on what anthropology can do to shed light on the human conundrum. It goes without saying that many people are as confident of anthropology's point of view as they are doubtful of the viewpoint to be described next.

This second point of view is that of *theosophy*. It is not our intention here to explore whether the choice of this word is fortunate or unfortunate; we shall simply use it to designate a second perspective on the study of human beings that is in contrast to that of anthropology.

Theosophy presupposes that human beings are, above all, spiritual beings and attempts to recognize them as such.[1] It sees the human soul, not only as "mirroring" and assimilating sense-perceptible things and processes, but also as capable of leading a life of its own, a life that receives its impetus and content from what can be called the spiritual side. It refers to human beings as capable of entering spiritual as well as sense-perceptible domains. In the latter, our knowledge and understanding expand as we direct our senses to more and more things and processes and form concepts based on them. In the spiritual domain, however, acquiring knowledge takes place differently; there, the observing is done within our inner experience. A sense-perceptible object stands there in front of us, but a spiritual experience rises up from within us, as if from the very center of our individual being.

As long as we cherish the belief that this is simply something taking place within the soul itself, theosophy must indeed seem highly questionable, since this belief is not at all far from the belief that presupposes such experiences to be nothing more than a further distillation of what we have observed through sense perception. To persist in such a belief is possible only as long as we have not had compelling reasons to be convinced that, after a certain point, inner experiences, just like sense-perceptible facts, are in fact determined by a world external to the human

---

1. See page 82 ff. for an alternate version of the rest of this chapter.

personality. When this conviction is acquired, the existence of a spiritual "outer world" must then be recognized, just as we recognize a physical one. It will then become clear to us that, just as we are rooted in a physical world through our physical nature, we are related to a spiritual world through our spiritual nature. We will then find it comprehensible that information can be gathered from this spiritual world to help us understand the spiritual human being, just as anthropology gathers information through physical observation to understand the physical human being. We will then no longer doubt the possibility of researching the spiritual world.

Spiritual researchers transform their soul experience in such a way that the spiritual world can enter it. They shape certain inner experiences so that the spiritual world reveals itself in them. (How this happens is described in my book *How to Know Higher Worlds*.) Thus configured, soul life can then be described as "clairvoyant consciousness." This is not in any way to be confused with the plethora of current shady practices that also go under the heading of "clairvoyance."

Coming to inner experience in such a way that one or another fact of the spiritual world can reveal itself directly to the soul requires much time, self-denial, and inner effort on the part of the soul. However, it would be a fatal preconception to believe that these soul experiences can bear fruit only for those individuals who achieve direct experience through inner exertion of this sort. That is not the case. Once spiritual facts have come to light in this way, they have been "conquered" for the human soul. If the spiritual researcher who has discovered them communicates them to others, they can then become clear to any individual who listens with impartial logic and a healthy sense for the truth. We should not believe that a well-founded certainty in the facts of the spiritual world is possible only for clairvoyant consciousness. Each and every soul is attuned to recognize the truth spiritual researchers have discovered. If a spiritual researcher makes claims that are untrue, impartial logic and a healthy sense of truth will recognize this and reject them.

Directly experiencing spiritual knowledge requires complex inner paths and practices, but possessing this knowledge is indispensable for any soul desiring to be fully conscious of its humanity. Without such consciousness, a human life is no longer possible after a certain point in our existence.

Although theosophy is capable of supplying knowledge that satisfies the most important needs of the human soul, and although this knowledge can be recognized by a healthy sense of truth and sound logic, there will always be a certain gap between theosophy and anthropology. The possibility will always exist that we will be able to demonstrate theosophy's conclusions regarding the spiritual nature of the human being and then indicate how anthropology confirms *everything* theosophy says. But the road between one domain of knowledge and the other will be a long one.

It is, however, possible to fill in the gap. This can be seen as the aim of the following sketch of an *anthroposophy*. If *anthropology* can be likened to the observations of a traveler in the lowlands who gets an idea of the character of an area by going from place to place and house to house, and if *theosophy* can be likened to the view we get of the same area from the top of a hill, then *anthroposophy* can be likened to our view from the slope of the hill, where we still see all the various details, but they begin to come together to form a whole.

Anthroposophy will study human beings as they present themselves to physical observation, but in the practice of this observation it will try to derive indications of a spiritual foundation from the physical phenomena. In this way, anthroposophy can make the transition from anthropology to theosophy.

It should be expressly mentioned that only a very brief sketch of anthroposophy can be given here, as a detailed description would entail too much. This sketch is intended to consider the human being's bodily nature only inasmuch as it is a revelation of the spiritual. This is what is meant by *anthroposophy* in the narrower sense. This would then have to be accompanied by *psychosophy*, which studies the soul, and by *pneumatosophy*, which is concerned with the spirit. With that, anthroposophy leads over into theosophy itself.[2]

·   ·   ·   ·   ·

---

2. For this progression, see *The Wisdom of Man, of the Soul, and of the Spirit*, which was previously called *Anthroposophy, Psychosophy, and Pneumatosophy.*

Alternate version of page 78 ff:

Theosophy presupposes that human beings are, above all, spiritual beings and attempts to recognize them as such. For theosophy, the life that a human being leads in different circumstances, climates, or times is a revelation of the spiritual being. Theosophy attempts to recognize the different forms in which this spiritual being can reveal itself and to portray out of the spirit what anthropology seeks to understand through outer observation. Theosophy's view of this spiritual being is not put forth as an arbitrary claim. Like anthropology, it is based on facts, although, because of their nature, these facts are contested from many quarters. Theosophy speaks of the inner aspect of the human being as something that can be developed; it is not something fixed and finished. Theosophy sees this inner aspect as containing seeds that can begin to sprout. When they do, we do not merely experience inner realities but enter into a world that is no less external to us than the sense-perceptible world. Our inner experiences begin to transmit this external spiritual world to us. They are not an end in themselves but are the means by which we go from our own inner world to the outer world of the spirit, just as our senses are the means by which the sense-perceptible outer world becomes our inner soul world.

Naturally, our relationship to the spiritual outer world must be different from our relationship to the sense-perceptible one, whose essential form always presents itself to us in the same way, regardless of how we approach it.

What goes on in our inner world can in no way change the course of sense-perceptible reality. Things are completely different, however, when our inner life is meant to develop into an organ for observing the spiritual world. First of all, we must silence any personal whims. This requires quite specific prerequisites. Inasmuch as these prerequisites achieve the necessary degree of perfection only approximately, individuals will always have difficulty in coming to a consensus on what they experience in the spiritual world by developing their inner life. Spiritual researchers cannot reach an agreement as easily as scientists of the physical world can. This, however, does not change the fact that we can develop inner dormant seeds into organs that lead us into a spiritual world. Only those who refuse to acknowledge this fact will raise objections to research into the spiritual world on the basis that spiritual researchers do not agree with each other.

Thus, theosophy is based on inner human experiences. Once such experiences have been discovered by one human soul, they can be understood by all others who do not totally shut themselves off from understanding. There is a string that can then resonate with anything a more highly developed soul may experience. This means that the spiritual world is just as much a matter for communication from person to person as the sense-perceptible world is. Because sense-perceptible realities present themselves in the same way to the unbiased observation of all, agreement about them must prevail. Agreement on a reality in the spiritual world cannot be brought about by outwardly taking people to look at something, but agreement will always result among individuals who follow inner soul paths to the spiritual reality in question. Those who actually follow this soul path, and are furthermore concerned only with the truth, will not be confused by what different spiritual researchers may say. They know that the contradictions are all too easily explained by the difficulties that arise when all personal whims must be eliminated.

It is understandable that theosophy's point of view seems questionable to many people. As it appears in the cultural evolution of humanity, it rises above the experiences of immediate existence to highlights of spiritual research. Although those individuals who need the results of theosophy to experience satisfaction in life will greet it with profound interest, others will be of the opinion that it is impossible for human beings to develop capacities to reach such heights. While there are doubtless many paths linking the results of spiritual research to our immediate life, it is also true that these paths are long for those who are conscientious. That is why what theosophy has to say about the human being seems so distant in many respects from the conclusions of anthropology.

In what follows, a third point of view will be taken up, standing midway between anthropology and theosophy. The resulting perspective will be called *anthroposophy*. Unlike theosophy, it will not present the results of inner experiences directly and will not see the external aspect of the human being as a manifestation of what is spiritually human; rather, this manifestation itself is what we will have in view. We will observe the external nature of the human being living in the sense-perceptible world, but in doing so we will seek out the spiritual foundation by means of its manifestation. We will not, however, stop with describing the manifestation as it manifests in sense-perceptible reality, as anthropology does. If theosophy could be likened to standing on top of a mountain surveying the landscape, while anthropology is investigating down in the lowlands, forest by forest and house by house, then anthroposophy will choose its vantage point on the slope of the mountain, where individual details can still be differentiated but integrate themselves to form a whole.

Only a brief sketch of a science characterized in this way will be given here; almost everything will appear as no more than suggestions. In the not-too-distant future, two other sketches will be added to form a totality with this one. In what follows, only what relates to the bodily nature of the human being will be depicted. This is what will be called *anthroposophy* in the narrower sense. A second sketch dealing with the soul will be called *psychosophy*, while the third, dealing with the spiritual aspect of the human being, will be called *pneumatosophy*. With that we will arrive at the conclusions of theosophy, although by a different path than that taken by theosophy itself.

CHAPTER 2

THE HUMAN BEING
AS A SENSORY ORGANISM

We shall begin *anthroposophy* with an examination of the human senses. Through our senses, we enter on one side into a relationship with an external world. In talking about the senses, however, two things should be borne in mind. We will disregard for the moment how human beings enter the other outer world, the spiritual world described above. And we will also disregard for the moment the possibility of something spiritual lying behind what our senses observe. In speaking about the senses, our attitude toward the spirit should be one of waiting to see to what extent an *indication* of the spiritual results naturally from sensory observation. This spiritual aspect should be neither denied nor presupposed; we must *wait* and see if it shines in.

We are here looking not at the objects of sense observation but at our senses themselves, the human organs. Based on what our senses convey to us, we develop ideas about an outer world. This is how our knowledge of this outer world comes about. With regard to this knowledge, we can speak of truth and error. Does error arise in the domain of the senses or only in the domain where, through conclusions, memory, and so on, we formulate ideas about what our senses tell us? It is justified to speak of sensory deception. For example, if some irregularity in our ears or eyes causes a sound or a light impression to appear differently than it would appear if the organ in question had developed normally, this is a case of deception by the senses. Does this mean that Goethe is unjustified in saying, "You may boldly trust your senses; they will not let you see anything false if your sound reason keeps you awake"?[1] Goethe's statement immediately proves justified if we consider the following. An error brought about by understanding or memory has a different character than a sensory deception, because the latter can be corrected by sound reasoning. For instance, if, due to faulty eyesight, we mistake a tree for a person, we will be in error only if we do not correct our mistake and, taking the illusory person to be an enemy, attack the tree. An error in understanding is different because here our reason itself errs; therefore, it cannot correct its own mistake at the same time. Deceptions by the senses become real mistakes only through our reason. This is a necessary distinction, not mere pedantry.

---

1. In the fourth stanza of his poem "Vermächtnis,"

> Den Sinnen hast du dann zu trauen,
> Kein Falsches lassen sie dich schauen,
> Wenn dein Verstand dich wach erhält.

Literally: The senses you must trust then / They will let you see nothing false / If your reason keeps you awake. A slight misquotation by Rudolf Steiner is reflected in the English version. — TRANS.

In speaking about sense perception, many people are accustomed to listing five different types—seeing, hearing, smelling, tasting, and touching (or feeling). We cannot stop at these, however, because we also enter into relationships with the outer world that are different from how we relate to it through hearing or seeing, for instance. Contemporary anthropological science also speaks about senses in addition to those listed above. We need not go into which senses anthropology enumerates, but it should be mentioned that this is one of those gratifying instances in which a science based purely on sense-perceptible physical realities is forced through its own observations to come to views that coincide in part with what spiritual researchers conclude. More and more such points of contact will be established as time goes on, and, if good will prevails on both sides, a time will soon come when natural and spiritual research will each recognize the validity of the other.

In an anthroposophical light, all *that* may be called a human sense which induces the human being to recognize the existence of an object, being, or process in such a way as to justify placing its existence into the physical world.

Seen in this way, the sense that appears least specific and most general is the one we may call the *sense of life*. We really notice that this sense exists only when what we perceive with it disrupts the order of our physical being. Suppose we feel tired or fatigued. We do not hear tiredness, nor do we smell it, yet we perceive it in the same sense that we perceive a smell or a sound. This perception, whose object is our own physical existence, is to be attributed to the sense of life. Basically, it is always present when we are awake, even though it really becomes noticeable only when some disturbance is present. It is by means of this sense that we each perceive ourselves as space-filling, bodily selves.

Another sense, different from the sense of life, is the one through which we perceive movements we carry out. For example, we move a leg and perceive the movement. We will call the sense through which this perception occurs the *sense of self-movement.* The difference between this sense and the sense of life becomes evident when we consider that what we perceive with our sense of life is only what is present in our inner physical being without our doing anything. What the sense of self-movement perceives has an activity or a motion as a prerequisite.[2]

A third sense becomes apparent when we notice that we are able to stay in the same position with regard to up and down, right and left, and so on. This sense can be called the *sense of balance* or *static sense.* Its characteristic feature becomes evident when we consider that we need to be able to perceive our position in order to maintain ourselves as conscious beings within it. If our sense of balance is not working, we succumb to dizziness and fall over. An object that does not possess consciousness will maintain its position without perceiving it; it cannot become dizzy. In speaking of this sense, anthropology

2. Since Rudolf Steiner's time, science has coined terms for this— *kinesthesia,* or muscle sense. — TRANS.

refers to an organ in the human ear, to three little semi-circular canals in the inner ear. When these are injured, dizziness occurs.

Reviewing the characteristic features of the three senses enumerated above, we find that, through each of them, we perceive something about our own physical existence. By means of the sense of life, we receive general sensations about our bodily existence; by means of the sense of self-movement, we perceive changes in this bodily existence; and, by means of the sense of balance, we perceive our relationship to the external spatial world—which, however, is disclosed to us as our position, as something belonging to our own physical condition. These three senses give us a feeling for our own bodily existence as a totality, which is the basis of our awareness of ourselves as physical beings. We may say that, through the senses of life, self-movement, and balance, the soul opens its doors to our own bodily existence and perceives this as the physical external world nearest to it.

With the senses to be considered next, we encounter an outer world that does not belong to us in the same way. The first sense we will consider here is the one that brings us into closest contact with what we call *matter*. Only gaseous or airy masses permit this close contact, which is conveyed to us through the *sense of smell*. A substance cannot be perceived by means of the sense of smell unless it is very finely dispersed and spreads like a gas.

At the next stage of sense perception, we no longer perceive merely the substance as such, but effects (actions) of the material element. This happens through the *sense of taste*. Only a watery mass, or one that has been dissolved in the fluid in our mouth, can be perceived by this sense. Through the sense of taste, we penetrate one stage deeper into outer substantiality than we did through the sense of smell. In smelling, the substance itself approaches us and discloses its particular character. In tasting, it is the substance's effect on us that is perceived. The difference between them is best felt by visualizing how, in the sense of smell, a gas-like substance approaches us in a finished state so that we can perceive it as it is, while, in the sense of taste, we use our own fluid to dissolve the substance—that is, we cause a change in it—in order to delve into peculiarities of this substance that it does not reveal to us on its own. This means that the sense of smell is suited to perceiving the outside of the material element, while the sense of taste already, to some extent, goes inside material things. For the inside of an object to be disclosed, we must change its outside.

The next sense, the *sense of sight*, allows us to delve still more deeply into the physical outer world. Whether we see a mass as red or blue divulges more to us about its *inside* than is contained in the effect conveyed to us by the sense of taste. It depends on the essential nature of an object whether it relates to colorless sunlight in a way that makes it seem red or blue under the influence of the light. Color is revealed as the outer surface of a mass. However, we can say that how a mass reveals itself on its surface is its inner nature becoming visible through the medium of light.

The *sense of warmth* delves still more deeply, down under the surface of a mass, so to speak. When we feel a piece of ice or a warm object, the cold or warmth is clearly not something that appears merely on the outer surface, like color, but something that permeates the object. Note that the sequence of senses described here is such that with each consecutive sense we dive down more *deeply* into the body of the outer world.

The *sense of hearing* constitutes another step in this direction. It leads into the interior of a body to a much greater extent than the sense of warmth. Sound makes a body's inwardness start to tremble. It is more than merely metaphorical to say that a body's soul comes to manifestation through sound. Through the warmth contained in a body, we experience something of the difference between it and its surroundings, but through sound its particular inner nature, its individual aspect, steps forth and communicates itself to our perception.

If we speak of a *sense* whenever cognition comes about without involvement of reason, memory, and so forth, we must acknowledge other senses in addition to the ones that have been enumerated so far. On the basis of this distinction, we can easily recognize that the word *sense* is often inappropriately used in everyday life, as when we say "sense of imitation," "sense of secrecy," and so forth. Our reason and judgment are already involved in what emerges as imitation, secrecy, and so on. In these instances, we are dealing with more than mere sense activity.

It is a different matter, however, when we hear speech and we perceive what is revealed through its tone.[3] It goes without saying, of course, that a complex evaluating activity comes into play in grasping what is spoken and that this involves extensive mental processes that cannot be encompassed by the term *sense*. But, in this domain, too, there is something simple and direct that *precedes* using mental judgment and that constitutes a sensation, just like a color or a degree of warmth. A phonetic tone is not perceived merely as sound, but, accompanying the sound, something much more inward is apprehended. If we say that within sound the soul of a body abides, then we can further say that in tone the soul manifests detached, freed from the bodily aspect, and thus appears with a certain independence. Because the sensation of phonetic tone precedes using mental judgment, children learn to sense the meaning of the tone of words before they can use judgment. In fact, they learn judgment by way of language. It is completely justifiable therefore to speak of a special *sense of tone* or *sense of word*. We have difficulty recognizing this sense only because, as a rule, so many different mental judgments accompany the direct sensation of what reveals itself in tone. But careful reflection on our

---

3. Steiner differentiates between *Ton* and *Laut* in the original German. *Ton* is translated as "sound," *Laut* as "tone" or "phonetic tone." The word "tone" is not used here primarily in the musical sense, but in the sense of *feeling-tone* in language, as used by Henry Head in his *Aphasia and Kindred Disorders of Speech,* Cambridge, 1926 (cited by Oliver Sacks in his essay on the sense of word, "The President's Speech," in *The Man Who Mistook His Wife for a Hat*). — TRANS.

own experience shows that, whenever we listen to what is given to us in tone, our relationship to the being from which the tone issues is as direct and free of judgment as is the case when we perceive an impression of color. Insight into this fact comes more easily when we recall how a cry of pain allows us to directly co-experience the pain of another being even before this perception mingles with any sort of reasoning or the like.

We must also take into account that audible tone is not alone in revealing to us an inwardness such as that present in tone of speech. In the end, gestures, mimicry, and facial expressions also lead us to something simple and direct that must be included, along with the content of any audible tone, in the domain of the sense of word.

The sensory character of the next sense to be described is concealed to an even greater degree. When we understand a person who is communicating by means of the spoken word, gestures, and so forth, it is primarily our judgment, memory, and so on, that are at work in this understanding. Accurate self-reflection, however, will lead us to recognize that in this case, too, there is a direct grasp or understanding that can precede any thinking or conclusion-drawing. The best way to get a feeling for this is to clarify for ourselves how we are able to understand something we are not yet even capable of judging or evaluating. Indeed, there also exists a *direct and immediate perception* for that which is revealed in a concept, so that we must speak of a *sense of concept*. What we can experience within our own soul as a concept, we can also receive as revealed from an external being.

In perceiving a concept, we delve even more deeply into a being than we do through perceiving the ensouled tone it makes. In fact, it is not possible through sense perception to delve more deeply into another being than we do through sensing what lives in that being as concept. Thus the sense of concept appears as the sense that penetrates the most inward aspect of another being. With the concept that lives within another human being, we perceive what lives, soul-like, within ourselves.

The sensory character of what is usually called the *sense of touch* does not appear in the same way as that of the ten senses already described here. The sense of touch conveys to us pressure or resistance from outside, hardness or softness. Let us recall the nature of what we call "pressure." The process is by no means a simple one. In reality, we do not perceive the object applying the pressure directly; rather, we perceive the fact that it makes us draw back with some particular part of our skin, or that we have to make a greater or lesser effort in order to make an impression on it. There is a remarkable difference between this perception and, for example, our perception of the degree of warmth an object reveals. Although it is true that a cold bath will feel different to someone who is overheated than it does to someone who is freezing—that is to say, our subjective condition is perceived along with the perception of warmth—it is nonetheless true that, for all practical purposes, the state of the external object is what is revealed in its warmth. This results in a direct and immediate relationship of the sensing person to the condition of the object. This is not how it is when we say that we have to make more or less of an effort to make an impression on an external object or to overcome the resistance its hardness or softness presents. What we are describing in this case is an inner experience we have due to an external body.

In actuality, although this is generally concealed, conclusion-drawing secretly accompanies our perception: "I am encountering considerable resistance; therefore, this body is hard." It is true that the perceptions of our sense of word can be totally direct and immediate, without any evaluating going on at all, but our sense of touch is always underlain by a judgment, even though it may be thoroughly concealed. What is *directly* felt through the sense of touch can always be found in the domain of the first three senses enumerated here. For example, a body that presses on me causes a change in position within my bodily makeup, and this change is perceived by means of my sense of life, my sense of self-movement, or my sense of balance.

We must keep the difference between the domains of the various senses clearly in mind, because we enter into a different relationship to external objects through each sense. Through the senses of life, self-movement, and balance, we delve into our own bodily nature and experience ourselves as beings of the outer world. Through the senses of smell, taste, and sight, the bodily aspect manifests itself to the extent that it reveals itself outwardly. It reveals inwardness through the sense of warmth, but still in an external way. With the help of our senses of hearing, word, and thought, we perceive an inwardness that is external to us. If we recognize the differences between these sensory domains, we will be less tempted to speak in generalities about what a sense is or what sense perception is. Instead, we will pay more attention to how we enter into a specific relationship to the outer world through each different sense. Describing sensory perception as an impression that is called up in the soul as a direct result of stimulating sensory nerves does not say much. Definitions like this make it all too easy for the character of each individual sense to get lost in vague generalizations. It is important, however, that our impression of a body's warmth is of a totally different character than the impression caused by light. If we do not take this into account, we will be easily misled into placing great value on statements such as, "Human beings perceive the outer world through their senses and develop ideas and concepts based on these sense perceptions." This sets up a simple contrast between sense perception and conceptual thinking. Drawing conclusions like this obscures our much-needed independent view of the fact that the sense of smell, for example, is very far removed from conceptual experience, while the sense of hearing facilitates sense perception that is already becoming similar to what is present within the soul as a conceptual experience.

CHAPTER 3

THE WORLD
UNDERLYING THE SENSES

Our sense perceptions provide the basis for the rest of our soul life. Mental images arise from our interaction with the outer world, based on the first three senses and also on smells, tastes, colors, sounds, and so on. Through these images, what comes to us from outside is mirrored in our souls. An ordering takes place that allows us to orient ourselves in this outer world. Experiences of sympathy and antipathy take form, and our feeling life takes shape within them; our wishes, urges, and willing develop.

A common identifying feature for this inner life of the human soul can only be found by looking at how it is held together and permeated, as it were, by what we each call our own *I*. A sensory perception becomes a soul experience when it is taken up out of the senses' domain and into the realm of the I. We can get an idea of this by pursuing the following simple line of thinking.

I feel, for example, the warmth of a certain object. As long as I touch the object, an interrelationship is present between my I and the outer world. Within this interrelationship, an image of the object's state of warmth develops in my I. When I take my hands off the object, this image remains in my I and constitutes something essential

within my soul life. We must not fail to note that it is precisely this image that frees itself from sensory experience
and goes on living in the soul. Within certain limits, we
can call these experiences, which we have with the help of
our senses and persist in our soul, "our world."

However, if we ponder how this world enters our
domain, we are forced to presuppose another existence
for it. How can this world ever become soul experience?
How can we know anything about it? Simply by virtue of
the fact that we have senses. Before the world can present
itself to human beings as sensory perception, the senses
themselves must be born out of it. The world would be
soundless for us if we had no sense of hearing, without
warmth if we had no sense of warmth. On the other hand,
it is equally clear that no sense of hearing could come
about in a world in which there was nothing to hear, no
sense of warmth in a world without warmth. We need
consider only the fact that no eyes develop in beings who
live in darkness, or the fact that eyes developed under the
influence of light degenerate when their owners give up
their existence in the light to dwell in darkness.

We need only to think this through in all clarity to be able
to say that the world presented to us through our senses, the
world on which we base our soul life, must be underlain by
another world, a world out of which the senses arise,
thereby making the sense world itself possible. This other
world cannot possibly fall within the domain of the sense
world, since it must precede it entirely.

This relationship of the senses to the world that gives
rise to them opens up to our contemplation the view of

another world lying behind the sense world, a world that is imperceptible to our senses, but out of which the sense world rises as if out of a sea of existence lying behind it. Our sense of warmth perceives warmth; behind the warmth lies something that has shaped our sense of warmth. Our eyes perceive by means of light; behind the light lies something that has shaped our eyes. We must distinguish between the world that is given to us through our senses and another world that underlies it. Is there anything we can say about this second world simply on the basis of reflection? Indeed, there is. Through our interrelationship with the outer world as conveyed to us in sense perception, our inner world of concepts, feelings, and desires comes about. Our relationship to the other world that we are presupposing underlies the sense world can be thought of in exactly the same way—through it, our sense organs come about.[1] We are present with our I in everything there is to experience in the sense world, and our soul world develops within the I on the basis of sensory experiences. The process of building up our sense organs, that necessarily precedes all sense perception, must take place in a domain of reality that no act of sense perception can penetrate. (We scarcely need to consider an objection that might arise in passing, specifically, that we can observe the development of sense organs in another being. What we can perceive in this case is perceived by means of our senses. We can

---

1. An alternate version of the following text can be found in the Appendices, beginning page 171.

observe how a hammer comes about without using a hammer ourselves, but we cannot possibly have a sensory perception of the development of a sense organ without ourselves making use of one.)

We are totally justified in saying that our sense organs must be built up out of a world that is itself *supersensible* [beyond sense perception]. And the nature of sense perceptions, as described in the previous chapter, provides a starting point for us to contemplate this other world and say more about it. Since our sense organs ultimately appear as the result of this world's activity, this activity must be manifold, working on us from as many different sides as we have sense organs. The streams from this world pour themselves into those wellsprings that lie in the sense organs, so that we may draw from them for our soul life. And because what we draw from these wellsprings is finally gathered together into the I, so it must, although coming from many sides, originally well up from something that is unified in its activity. The manifold sense perceptions are unified in the I. In this unity, they show that they belong together.

What impinges on the soul as sense perceptions is such that the inner life of the I can separate itself out from them. From this it is apparent that, in a supersensible world behind the sense world, there exist as many springs of activity as there are sense organs. These springs of activity reveal themselves through their *working* in the building up of the sense organs.

Thus, the number of these wellsprings of activity is equal to the number of our sense organs. The outermost limits of the realm of these wellsprings can be assumed to be set by the I on the one hand and the sense of touch on the other, although neither of these may be reckoned as belonging to our sensory life as such. Once something belongs to the I, it has freed itself from sense perception and should no longer be counted as such, since it is now a wholly inner experience. But intrinsic to *any* sense perception is the fact that it can become an I-experience. Therefore, every sense organ must have been endowed by the supersensible world with the ability to provide something that can become an I-experience. But the sense of touch provides experiences of the opposite sort, so to speak. Whatever it tells us about an object is presented as something wholly external to us. Thus, we ourselves in our entirety must have been built up out of the supersensible world in such a way as to use experiences of touch to set ourselves apart from a world lying outside us.

If we survey human soul life as it develops on the basis of sensory experiences, our sense organs appear as fixed points as if on the circumference of a circle, and the I appears as something movable that acquires soul experiences as it moves through this circle in different ways. The human organism's entire structure—at least as it reveals itself in the sense organs—points to its origins in the supersensible world. There are as many sensory domains as origins and, within the realm of these origins, a unified supersensible principle that is pointed to by the orientation toward the unity of the I.

Further observation shows that the supersensible activity revealing itself in the structure of our sense organs works in a variety of ways. In the three domains of the senses of life, self-movement, and balance, it works from within our bodily existence outward and makes its presence known right up to the boundary of our skin. In the senses of smell, taste, sight, warmth, and hearing, this outward-directed activity is also present, but it is accompanied by another, which we must describe as working in the opposite direction, into our physical existence from outside. Consider, for example, the organ of hearing as a member of the human organism. Within this organism, forces must be present that actively shape this organ in accordance with the nature of the body as a whole. But there must also be supersensible forces coming from outside, forces that are concealed in the world of sound and that shape the organ in just the right way to make it receptive to sound.

The organs of the last five senses listed above point to a meeting of forces on the surface of the human body, as it were. Forces working from within the body outward configure our individual sense organs according to the nature of the body as a whole; while forces working from outside inward come to meet these inner forces and impress the organs on the body, in such a way that they adapt to the various expressions of the outer world. In the senses of life, self-movement, and balance, only one of these two directions—the one working from inside out— is present.

It becomes further apparent that, in the word sense and concept sense, the direction from within outward is absent. These senses are built into the human being from the outside in. The supersensible activity that shapes these senses is already becoming similar to our inner soul life.

To the extent that we must also already see the potential for the I in the supersensible forces that build up our senses (as described above), we can say that these forces divulge their inner nature to the greatest extent in the I. In the I, however, their inner nature has condensed into a point, so to speak. If we consider the I, it shows a reality in one point, which rests spread out in richest profusion in a supersensible world. This reality, working out of this supersensible world, reveals itself only in its effects, in building up our senses. The sense of touch shows itself to be the opposite of the I in this respect as well. In the sense of touch is revealed that aspect of the supersensible world—or, if you will, extra-supersensible world—that cannot become inner experience for the human being, but is inferred by means of corresponding inner experiences.

Anthropology describes our sense organs as sense-perceptible phenomena. The fact that it does not yet designate specific organs for the three senses of life, self-movement, and balance coincides with the results presented above, since the forces characterized as working from within outward shape the human individual into a sensory organism, which is general, which experiences itself, and which maintains its posture. The organs of these three sensory domains spread out over our general bodily existence. Only when it comes to the sense of balance does anthropology point to the three semicircular canals as a suggestion of a specific sense organ, because, with this sense, we enter into an elementary relationship with the outer world, specifically with the directions of space.

The five middle senses have separate organs. We can easily recognize that the capabilities we have described as working from within outward and from outside inward work together in various different ways to form these organs. (Anthropology still has some doubts about the existence of an outer sense organ for the sense of warmth, but these doubts will be resolved as science progresses.)

Outer organs for the sense of word and the sense of concept cannot be described in the same way as the organs for the other senses because these organs are already located where our bodily life turns inward to become soul life.

The sense of touch, however, will increasingly show itself to science as what it must indeed be in light of what has been considered above. It cannot but work in such a way that we draw back from the objects we are touching, withdrawing into ourselves—shutting ourselves off from the domains of this sense by shutting ourselves up in our inner bodily experiences. We consider the organs of the sense of touch to be structures spread out over the entire surface of the body, and we are thus obliged to recognize in these structures something that intrinsically has to do with the body's surface drawing back from the outer world it touches. The organs of touch, therefore, actually shape the inside of our human bodily form; they give the body the shape through which it closes itself off from the outer world touching it on all sides. (In areas where our organs of touch demonstrate greater sensitivity, we relate

differently to the outer world than we do in areas of lesser
sensitivity. We push against the outer world to a greater
or lesser extent, so to speak. This leads us to notice that in
some respects our bodily form is a result of the specific
nature of the organ of touch at different points on the surface of the body.)

CHAPTER 4

THE LIFE PROCESSES

Another type of activity plays into our sense life. Here, too, we can distinguish a number of different domains. The first to present itself is the process by which our body's inner life is supported from outside, namely our *breathing*. In the breathing process, our bodily life touches the outer world. It then receives from the outer world the strength it needs to continue. Our bodily life sets itself against the outer world in a way that it cannot maintain. These words more or less express that which can be said about what manifests itself to us about the breathing process without going into the results of sense-perceptible science. The latter belong to the field of anthropology. What has just been described is something we experience directly in our own life—in our own need for air, in observing how life is inhibited by lack of air, and so on.

A second process in this domain can be described as *warming*. To maintain bodily life, we must develop a certain degree of warmth in our body that does not depend on the warmth of our surroundings; rather the processes within the body maintain our own bodily warmth within certain limits—independent of how warm it is outside the body.

A third process of this type is *nourishing*. Through this process, the life of the body enters into a relationship with the outer world so that the substances we have used are replaced. However, a fourth process must take place for the process of nourishing to occur. Already in the mouth, the food that is taken in must begin interacting with saliva secreted by the body, and a process of this sort continues to take place as digestion proceeds. This process can be seen as the fourth in this domain, and can be called *secreting*.

Observing our own bodies shows us that another process is connected with this one. In the secreting that serves the digestive process, the secreted substance is only capable of transforming our food so that it can enter into the life of the body. But it must also be possible to secrete substances that can become part of this bodily life. We must transform nutrients so that they can serve to build up the body. This is based on a process that goes beyond what has been characterized as secreting. We will call this the process of *maintaining*.

Yet another process becomes evident when we turn our attention to the growth of the human being. This transcends the process of maintaining, which would leave the body as it is at a certain point in time. An additional process is needed, one we can describe as the process of *growing*.

The processes of maintaining and growing reach their culmination when the completed human body takes on its very specific form. This taking shape of the human being, coming from within and culminating in a specific form, will be called the process of *generating*.

Reproduction can be seen as a repetition of this generating. What belongs to the individual body is generated in such a way that it remains united with the individual, while, in the case of reproduction, what is generated does not. Since we are concerned here, to begin with, only with the individual human being as a self-contained bodily entity, we will not take the reproductive process into account.

The processes that we have called *breathing*, *warming*, *nourishing*, *secreting*, *maintaining*, *growing*, and *generating* now are linked to inner experiences similar to the inner experiences in the I that link up with the processes of sensory perception. Breathing, warming, and nourishing are linked to emotional experiences that, under normal conditions, we are scarcely aware of, but immediately become prominent when the normal state is disturbed in one direction or the other. If breathing cannot proceed in the appropriate fashion, feelings of anxiety and similar feelings appear. A disturbance in the state of warmth announces itself in our feeling chilly or overheated. A disturbance in nourishing reveals itself in our feeling hungry and thirsty. We can say that the inner experiences linked to breathing, warming, and nourishing manifest in a sort of well-being or comfort. These experiences are always present; when a disturbance occurs, they are the basis for what comes to expression as feeling unwell, discomfort, hunger, and so on.

Genuine reflection on our own experience shows that similar feeling-like experiences are also associated with the processes of secreting, maintaining, growing, and generating. If we think about how excessive perspiration can signal a state of anxiety or fear, we will be able to acknowledge that, when secretion of this sort stays within reasonable bounds, it is associated with a feeling that expresses itself as comfort of a general sort, and we can also see that all secreting is accompanied by a state of feeling that, as long as it is proceeding normally, escapes conscious observation. Further self-reflection shows that such feeling experiences are also associated with the processes of maintaining, growing, and generating. We can sense, for instance, that teenagers' feelings of power are the expression of inner experiences linked to the process of growth.

These inner feeling experiences come to face the processes of breathing, warming, growth, and so on, in a way that is similar to how, in the I, the inner experiences arising in the wake of sense perceptions come to face the sensory processes. Thus it is possible to say, for example, that the relationship of breathing to a certain inner experience is similar to the relationship of hearing to the experience we call sound, although outer sense perceptions reverberate inwardly with a much greater degree of clarity than the other experiences just described.

Concealed, so to speak, under or within our *I-human being*,[1] is another human being who is built up out of such inner experiences just as our I-being is built up of our experiences of external sense impressions. This

---

1. The German *Ich-Mensch*—literally "I-human being"—has generally been translated in this text simply as "I-being." — TRANS.

other human being is, however, really only taken notice of in life when its experiences are disturbed, causing it to make its presence known to the I-human being. We are, however, no more justified in lumping together the breathing process, for example, and the inner experiences accompanying it, which are feeling-like in character, than we would be in lumping together the process of sense perception with the related process taking place in the I.

We could easily be tempted to fail to recognize the particular character of these inner experiences and conclude that there is no significant difference between them and the ones that develop under the influence of sense impressions. Admittedly, the difference between these two types of inner experience—for example, between our sense of life and our inner, feeling-like experiences with regard to the processes of breathing or warming—is not particularly clear. However, this difference can be ascertained easily through more precise observation if we keep the following in mind.

Inherent in a sensory experience is the fact that a judgment can be connected to it only through the I. Everything we do under the influence of a judgment relating to sense perceptions must be such that we arrive at this judgment within the I. If, for example, a flower is perceived and judged to be beautiful, the I inserts itself between our perception and our judgment. The inner experiences called up by processes of breathing, warming, nourishing, and so on, indicate in and by themselves something similar to judgment, without the I coming in between. In the experience of hunger lies a direct indication of something, which corresponds to hunger, and which is connected with the hunger in the same way as that which the human being connects with a sense perception after having formed a judgment with regard to this sense perception. When we arrive at judgments relating to a sense perception, the activity of the I brings something together with the sense perception. Similarly, we see that something external to hunger has been connected with hunger, but without the I bringing about this connection. Thus, we may call this latter connection an *instinctive* manifestation. This holds true for all inner experiences related to the processes of breathing, nourishing, growing. Therefore, we must distinguish between comfort in breathing, well-being in warmth—to the extent that these are instinctive inner experiences—and the corresponding perceptions of the sense of life. To gain access to the domain of the sense of life, the wave of instinct must first wash up against the I-being, so to speak.

The framework of these inner experiences that take place behind the "I-human being" through the processes described here will be attributed to the "astral human being."[2] For the moment, we will associate nothing more with this term than what is described here. The I-being draws its experiences from the sense world by means of the instruments of our senses, while the astral being draws its experiences from the world given in the processes of

---

2. The German here is *astraler Mensch* — "astral human being." Sometimes, in what follows, it has been translated simply as "astral being." — TRANS.

breathing, growing, and so on. For the moment we will call this world "the world of life."

The forces building up our sense organs transcend what is sense perceptible. Similarly, for a world of life to exist, the organs of life must be constructed out of a world that transcends all life. Also, this world reveals itself in its effects: the building up of the organs of life. The distinct domains of the life processes—breathing, warming, nourishing, and so on—may be taken to indicate an equal number of domains in this world.

It can be further noticed that the domains of the individual life processes are less strictly separated from each other than are the domains of sense perception. The domain of the sense of smell, for example, is strictly separated from the sense of sight, whereas the domains of the life processes are closer together; they intermingle more. Breathing merges into warming, warming into nourishing.

Thus, anthropology points to essentially separate organs for sense perception, while for the life processes it points to organs that flow into one another. The lungs, the primary breathing organ, are connected to the organs of blood circulation, which serve the process of warmth, while these in turn flow together with the organs of digestion, which correspond to the process of nourishing, and so on.

This indicates that, in the world in which the forces building up these organs are found, the relationships among the corresponding domains are different from the relationships among the forces that build up the sense organs. The former relationships must be more mobile than the latter. The experiences of the sense of taste, for example, can meet the experiences of the sense of hearing only in the common I to which they belong. The feeling of growing, on the other hand, automatically encounters what presents itself in the breathing process. The feeling of strength associated with growing shows up in our comfort in breathing, warming, and so on, through a heightened inner life. Each experience of feeling of this kind can concur with a different one of the same kind. As we saw in the case of the sensory domains, we could use the image of a circle on which the individual domains were located, while the I moved through all of them. But from what we have seen thus far, a different image results with regard to the life processes. We can imagine each of these as being mobile and each one capable of superimposing itself on any of the others.

There are also clear relationships between our sense perceptions and our life processes. Let us consider the process of breathing as it relates to perceiving sound. In both cases, the corresponding bodily organ encounters the outer world. This indicates that what is revealed in the outer world relates to both. But it becomes evident that in the air, for example, two different things are revealed. One relates to how the organ of breathing takes shape and is placed in the service of the body, while the other relates to the structure of the organ of hearing. This allows us to realize that the forces shaping the organ of hearing must, in a certain sense, be of earlier origin than the ones shaping the organ of breathing. In the fully formed human body everything is interdependent. A human organ of hearing can develop from the inside outward only if the organ of breathing is predisposed exactly as it shows itself to be. Both the organ of breathing and the organ of hearing grow from inside the organism outward toward the external world, but the organ of breathing needs to be adapted only to the internal life of the body, while the organ of hearing has to be adapted to the other world, the realm of sound. When the organ of breathing grows outward from the body, only the constitution of the body itself needs to be taken into account; the organ of hearing, however, must grow outward in such a way as to be adapted to the external world of sound. Nothing needs to precede the potential breathing organ; it grows in accordance with inner formative forces. The organ of hearing, however, must grow in the direction of an already existing tendency; its adaptation to the outer world must precede its unfolding out of the inner life of the body.

This shows that the forces that shape the organ of hearing into a sense instrument belong to a world that is of earlier origin or higher than the world where the forces are to be found that show themselves as the ones shaping, from inside the body outward, both the organ of hearing and the organ of breathing.

Something similar can be demonstrated with regard to other sense perceptions and life processes. Let us consider the sense of taste, which we can relate to secreting just as we related the sense of hearing to the breathing process. The saliva in the mouth contains what is needed to dissolve our food and make it capable of being tasted. A train of thought similar to that followed above can show that the forces from which the organs of secretion take shape are of later origin than those through which the sense of taste comes about.

In line with these considerations, we can therefore presuppose the existence, within the human being, of a supersensible higher being, whose forces manifest in the activity of building up the human sense organs. Similarly, we may presuppose another supersensible being, whose activities manifest in the building up of the human organs of life. The world of the latter is felt by the astral human being as his instinctive inner experiences, while the world of the former reveals itself to the I-human being as sense-perceptible reality (the sense world) [indirectly]. But neither can the world of the first supersensible being become directly manifest through the senses, nor can the world of the second come to a direct manifestation in the astral human being.

We have said that, in the I, the supersensible world reveals itself in its intrinsic character as if condensed into one point. Similarly, we can recognize that in receiving feeling experiences that result from life processes, the astral human being receives the revelation of a supersensible world in which the organs of these processes (the life organs) acquire the essential character of (1) serving life, and (2) forming the sense organs out of themselves. These experiences are the expression of something with which the other instinctive experiences of the "astral being" flow together into one, revealing their greatest effectiveness as a shape-forming force. [3]

3. See page 119 for an alternate version of this paragraph.

The I-human being and the astral being represent two parts of the human being which are active in inner processes. To make the I-human being possible, the forces of a supersensible world build up the sense organs. To the extent that the human body is the bearer of the sense organs, it shows itself to be built up out of a supersensible world. We will call this bearer of the sense organs the *physical human body*. The I-human being permeates it in order to live, with its help, in the sensory world. Thus we must see the physical human body as an entity built out of forces that are intrinsically related to the I itself. Within the sensory world, the physical human body can show itself only in its sense-perceptible manifestation; but, in its inner reality, it is an entity of a supersensible sort.

To make the astral being possible, a supersensible world builds up the organs of life. As we have seen, this world's forces are related to the astral human being's experiences. What builds up the physical being is revealed in the sensory world in the way described above. The forces that build up the organs of life can reveal themselves only in the instinctive feeling experiences stemming from the life processes, for they do not produce any sense organs, and only sense organs can give evidence of sense-perceptible things. The organs of life themselves are not organs of perception. Therefore, not only do the forces that build up the organs of life remain imperceptible to the senses, but also their manifestation in the human being cannot become sense-perceptible; it can only be a feeling-like instinctive experience. This manifestation will be called the *etheric human body*.

("Etheric" in this sense refers only to what is meant here, and not to what is given the name "ether" in physics.) The etheric human body relates to the astral human being as the physical human body relates to the I-human being.[4]

The physical body is so constituted as to convey the experiences of the senses to the I; the ether body can be only indirectly and instinctively experienced by the astral human being. The I must relate to the physical human body as the astral human being relates to the etheric human body. Thus, the life processes presuppose the existence of forces to which they adapt in shaping sense organs, such as the organ of hearing, from within the body outward to correspond to experiences which they themselves do not serve. The sense organs, in turn, since they are supported by the life processes, presuppose the existence of the organs of life.

To the extent that it is the bearer of the sense organs, the physical human body is formed out of the higher spiritual world, and, to the extent that it builds up the organs of life, the etheric human body is formed out of the lower spiritual world. In the astral world, the astral human being enters into relationship with the life processes to the extent that they are revealed in our life instincts. In the physical world, the I-human being enters into relationship with the sense experiences that present themselves as the outer world (tone, sound, warmth, light, and so on), to the extent that these reveal themselves as the sensory world.

---

4. See page 119 ff. for an alternate version.

. . . . .

Alternate version of page 116:

We have said that, in the I, the supersensible world reveals itself in its intrinsic character as if condensed into one point. In the same sense, we can recognize that the second world described here shows itself in those feeling experiences of the astral human being that can be termed the life instincts. These experiences are an expression of something that flows together and forms a unity with the astral human being's other instinctive experiences, and are an image of a supersensible world in the same sense that the I-human being is an image of another such world.

. . . . .

Alternate version of page 117:

In order to make it possible for the astral human being to exist, another world, the world of life, exists in addition to the supersensible world we have characterized here and builds up the organs of life. As we have seen, the forces of this world are related to what the astral human being experiences in the life instincts. As described above, what builds up the physical human being reveals itself in the sense world. In the physical world, the forces that build up the organs of life can reveal themselves only in the life processes, for they create the life organs, which are the only means by which a life process can reveal itself. The life organs themselves are not organs of perception. For this reason, both the forces that build up the organs of life and the manifestation of these forces in the human being remain imperceptible to the senses. We will call this manifestation the "etheric human body." (We must think of the term "etheric" only in the sense of what is meant here, and not in the sense of what physics terms the "ether.") The etheric human body relates to the astral human being in the same way that the physical human body relates to the I-human being. By its very nature, the physical body is constituted in such a way that it makes itself sense-perceptible; the etheric body, however, as the producer of the life organs, can be experienced only indirectly and instinctively by the astral human being.

Thus, we can distinguish:

1) A supersensible world in which the forces for building up the sense world are present.

2) A supersensible world in which the forces for building up the life organs are to be found. This presupposes the existence of the first supersensible world. Therefore we may call the first the higher spiritual world, the second the lower spiritual world.

3) A world in which the astral human being relates to the life processes in such a way that they disclose themselves as the life instincts. This presupposes the existence of life processes, that is, of the second world, and will be called the astral world.

4) A world in which sensory experiences disclose themselves to the I-human being by means of the sense organs. This is the physical world, the sense world.

CHAPTER 5

PROCESSES IN THE
INNER HUMAN BEING

In the preceding chapter, we considered the astral being only from the point of view of how it appears in feeling-like experiences as a sort of reflection of the processes of our life organs. These experiences, however, are not the only ones that belong to the astral human being. To these we must add, first of all, our *capacity for movement*. We do not move only in response to impulses occurring as a result of the life processes. Our impulses for movement lie in our inner life, insofar as this is independent of the life processes. But self-reflection will show that the impetus for these impulses certainly does not always come from the I-human being. Rather, these impulses for movement generally present themselves as instinctive experiences and therefore belong to the same domain as the instinctive experiences that are linked to the life processes. That is, they belong to the astral being.

In addition, what can be called instinctive *desires* also appear as experiences belonging to the astral being. Desires come about as the result of sense perceptions. But self-reflection shows that, when sensory perception is taken up by the I-being, it first leads to a judgment. This judgment then works on the astral being when a desire arises. Within the I-being, the following experience takes shape: what is being perceived is valuable; our interest in it is awakened. If this interest is then to become a desire, the judgment must be taken up by an impulse coming from the astral human being. Desires also develop on the basis of experiences related to the life processes. The feeling-like experiences described earlier are, however, not yet desires. The experience of hunger, for example, is not yet a desire; similar to a judgment, it merely points our attention to the corresponding life process. The actual desire is an independent experience which the astral human being adds to the feeling of hunger. There are also desires that have their roots in the astral being, without incitement from the life processes or outer perceptions. Certain drives belong to the domain from which such desires spring.

A third type of independent experience belonging to the astral human being arises when we reflect on how something inserts itself between the process of sensory perception and the I-being's experience. This is the "image" that arises out of the interplay between sensory experience and the I, based on the former. Sensory experience is transient, lasting only as long as the sense organ in question is focused on the object. The image remains, however; but this "image" does not, in itself, belong to judgment, to the activity of the I. judgment bases itself on this image. The image comprises an experience of the astral being, not of the I-being. We can also call this image a *sensation* if we take this term to refer to the content of a sensory experience rather than the experience itself. In this sense of the word, *sensations* are the astral human being's third type of independent experience.

In the same way that we speak of sense organs with regard to the physical being and life organs with regard to the etheric being, we can speak of impulses for movement, of desires, and of sensations with regard to the astral human being. Again, the organs for these experiences cannot originate in the astral human being itself, because the astral being must possess these organs before it can make these experiences possible. The organs must be formed out of a world lying outside of the astral human being. Because the impulses for sensation, desire, and movement are rooted in the astral human being itself, which is in a way an observer of what must develop within it, the forces shaping the organs in question can originate only in the sphere in which the entire astral human being originates. This, therefore, presupposes the existence of a world that, although lying outside it, is of the same essential nature as the astral human being.

The nature of this world can again reveal itself by means of the astral human being's innermost experience. This we can recognize to be the "sensations" or "image sensations" in the sense described above. In our desires and impulses for movement, we see, however, something that points beyond this inner experience. Our desires and our impulses for movement must be roused from a world similar to the world of images, whose unfolding we witness as astral human beings.

We can distinguish between the astral human being as it experiences itself inwardly in images, desires, and impulses for movement, and the astral human being as the revelation of a world lying outside of desires and impulses for movement. In order to distinguish the second astral human being from the first, we will call the second the "astral body." Like the ether body, it cannot be perceived by our senses because it does not generate organs of physical perception, but only of sensation, desire, and impulse for movement. It is immediately clear that desire and impulse for movement cannot convey sensory perception; but we must recognize that this is also true of sensation insofar as it is of the same nature as the forces that build up the astral body. For also the image that comes about by means of a sense experience detached from this experience persists as content of the astral human being. The forces that shape the organs of the astral human being must be thought of as similar to a detached image, and not as a sense-perceptible experience. As long, however, as we think of this image as deriving its content from a sense experience, it cannot be used to illustrate the forces out of which the astral body takes shape. In order for *such* an image to come about, a sense organ is necessary. It must be an image of the same sort, but of different origin. An image of fantasy is of this sort. But as long as an image of fantasy originates in the merely personal whim of the I-human being, it naturally cannot be considered to characterize the world in question. It must emanate from a *reality* lying outside both the I-being and the astral being.

Taking all this into account, we can arrive at an idea of how the astral body must be constituted. It is, in line with the indications we have arrived at, a body of images rooted in reality, which enkindles out of itself the forces of desire and movement.

The domains corresponding to sensory experiences could have been pictured on a peripheral circle, on which those separate forces are distributed that manifest in the sense organs as their causes. In the domains corresponding to the life processes, we could have chosen the picture of the corresponding separate forces flowing over one another. We *must* describe them as "flowing over one another," because the individual life processes *do not interpenetrate*. Breathing, for example, is close to the process of maintaining, because the organ of breathing must continually be built up anew by the maintaining process. But, although the organ of breathing experiences the influence of the maintaining process, the process of breathing itself is not changed. Thus, the two processes of breathing and maintaining pass each other by.

This is different with the processes of movement, desire, and "image sensation." These three processes work as follows. Image sensations are effectively at work within desires; desires live on into the impulses for movement. We are therefore justified in saying that, when image sensation meets the force of desire, the former penetrates the latter, and the content of the image sensation lives on in the desire. In the same way, the desire— together with the image sensation—lives on in the movement. We can therefore picture the forces of the world out of which the astral body is formed as three force formations: the formation that corresponds to image sensations works on the formation that streams forth desires, while both the effects of the first two formations persist in the formation for movements.

It will now be easy for us to recognize that the world we have described here as the one in which the astral body originates is the same as the one described in the preceding chapter as the astral world. For the life processes must first transform themselves into life instincts before they can exist as impulses in the astral human being. Life instincts, image sensations, desires, and impulses for movement thus belong to the astral human being, to the extent that this astral being presupposes the existence of the lower spiritual world and has its own origin in the astral world.

CHAPTER 6

I-EXPERIENCE [1]

Within the human being's experience of the I itself lies nothing that is incited by a sensory process. On the other hand, the I assimilates the outcomes of the sensory processes into its field of experience, fashioning from them its particular structure of inwardness, the actual I-human being. This I-human being thus consists wholly of experiences that have their origin outside the I, yet outlast the corresponding sensory experiences by persisting within the I. These experiences can therefore be transformed into I-experiences.

We can acquire an idea of how this happens by observing the experiences of our so-called sense of touch. Here, nothing belonging to an object in the external world enters the I's experiences. The I sends its own being raying outward, so to speak, to the point of contact with the outer object, and then allows it to ray back into itself with the quality of what it touched. The I's own being—raying back—constitutes the content of the perception of touch.

---

1. An alternate version of this chapter appears in Appendix 2, page 188.

Now why does the I not immediately recognize this perception of touch as its own content? Because this content has received a counterthrust from the other side, from outside, and now returns corresponding to the imprint it has received through the outer world's impact. The I content returns bearing an imprint that it has received from outside. The I thus receives into the structure of its own particular content a certain particularity of the outer world. That these are actually inner I-experiences that have merely received the imprint of the outer world's particularity can be ascertained only by means of a judgment.

Let us now assume that the I's experience could not accomplish making contact with the outer object. The object would send its own being raying outward, and the I's experience would have to recoil before touching the object. In this case, an experience similar to the experience of touch would come about within the I; but because of the weaker resistance that the I asserts in its experience, something like a flowing in of the outer will occur. The experience of smell, in fact, can be characterized as just such a process.

If the impact from outside is so strong that the object raying in from the outside digs into the I's experience, then an influx from outside can occur. Only when the inner experience begins—so to speak—to defend itself, can it "close itself up" against the particularity of the outer world. It has then, however, absorbed the influx from outside and now carries it within itself as proper inner being. The sense of taste can be characterized in this way.

If, however, the I confronts outer existence not with its primary self-experience, but with the essence of what it has assimilated from the outside, then a particularity from the outside can be imprinted into an inner experience that was itself originally taken in from outside. The outer world then makes its imprint on an inner experience which is itself an interiorized outer experience. This is how the sense of sight presents itself. In the sense of sight, it is as if the outer world were dealing with itself within the I's experiences. It is as if it had first sent a member of its own being into the human being, in order to then imprint its own particularity on this member.

Let us now further assume that the outer world fully fills, as it were, the I's experience with what it has sent inward as a sense organ; then the particularity of an outside will in sense experience reverberate in the inner, even though inner experience and outer world stand opposite one another. When the outer world then rays in, it reveals itself as equivalent to an inside. The I will experience outside and inside as equivalent in character. This is the case with the sense of warmth. Let us compare the experiences of the sense of warmth with the life process of warming. An impression of warmth must be recognized as something equivalent in character to the inwardly experienced warmth that fills the inside.

With the senses of smell, taste, and sight we can speak of a streaming in of the outer world into the I's experiences. Through the sense of warmth, the inner life is filled with the character of the outer world. A sense perception from within manifests through the senses of balance, self-movement, and life. Through them, the I experiences its inner physical fullness.[2]

Something different transpires in the case of the sense of hearing. There, the outer being does not merely allow our I-experiences to approach it as it does in the sense of touch, nor does it bore into our I-experiences as it does in the senses of smell, taste, and sight, but rather it lets itself be shone upon, as it were, by our I-experiences; it allows these to approach itself. Only then does it counter with its own forces. The I thereby experiences something like an expansion into the outer world, like a placing of the I-experiences outside. We can recognize a relationship like this in the case of the sense of hearing. (Only those given to abstract comparisons will object that such an expansion into the outer world also takes place in the sense of sight, for example. Our perception of sound is essentially different in character from our sense of sight. In color, I-experience as such is not present in the same sense that it is present in sound.) To an even greater extent, the expansion of I-experiences into the surroundings occurs through the sense of word and the sense of concept.

. . . . .

---

2. See below for alternate version of preceding two paragraphs.

Alternate version of text beginning on page 129:

Let us now further assume that the outer world fully fills, as it were, the I's experience with what it has sent inward; then everything inside will have the particularity of an outside, even though it is inner experience. When the outer world rays in, it reveals itself as equivalent to the inside. The I will experience outside and inside as equivalent in character. This is the case with the sense of warmth. An impression of warmth must be recognized as owing its existence to something equivalent in character to the warmth that is produced within and fills the inside. (Anthropology must acknowledge this, since it must think of inner warmth as coming about through inner combustion just as outer warmth comes about through combustion.) If we reflect on the body-filling result of outer warmth processes, this appears as a second type of inner experience, as something that fills the I and takes on the nature of the I within the I itself. Thus, something inserts itself into our I-experiences, filling the first I like a second I. This second I is, indeed, an I-experience over against the experience of the first I. But to the extent that only the first I really feels itself to be itself, it must conceive of this second I as an image sensation of itself. And that outer world in which the second I has its roots has fully become an inner world.

If we can speak of how the outer world streams into our I-experiences in the senses of smell, taste, and sight, we can also imagine the case in which a piece of the outer world that we recognize as having been interiorized not only works to fill up our inner life, as it does in the sense of warmth, but goes beyond a mere filling up to an over-growing[3] of our inner experiences. In this case, it would present itself like a sense perception from within. This, in fact, is the actual relationship with regard to the senses of balance, self-movement, and life. Through them, the I experiences its inner fullness.

---

3. The German *überwuchern* means literally "to overgrow," and figuratively, "to take over." — TRANS.

CHAPTER 7

THE WORLD UNDERLYING
THE SENSE ORGANS

To characterize the astral human being, we had to point to the trinity of image sensation, desire, and impulse for movement. The I-human being, to the extent that it is experienced directly in its sense processes, shows itself to be a unity. As our considerations have shown, all sensory experiences are only I-experiences in different modifications or gradations. In the experience of the I itself, the human being stands in direct relationship to the supersensible world. The other I-experiences are mediated through organs. And through these organs, the I-experiences manifest themselves in the multitude of the sensory domains.

Now two organs, the organs of the sense of thought and the sense of tone, allow to a certain degree an easy description of the unfolding of sensory capacity. When perceiving a concept, the previously acquired concepts prove to be what absorbs the new concept. We can understand a new concept that comes toward us to the extent that certain concepts have been absorbed previously. When understanding a concept, we must therefore open up to the outside and plunge what is received into the previously existing organism of concept. The life that unfolds there blossoms toward the outside and takes root in the organism of concept.

Something similar occurs with the sense of tone. We are receptive to a new meaning of a tone to the extent that we have already acquired other meanings of tone. We really do carry within ourselves an organism of concept and of tone. Both must be present before I-experiences can take place through them. The I-being cannot produce these organisms of tone and concept by means of forces present in sensory life. And yet a third is necessary. The I unfolds its experience toward all sides, so to speak, but, within this experience, cannot experience itself. In order to experience itself, it must confront itself with its own experience. It confronts itself with itself as sensation. We see that the sensation of I and the experiences of the sense of concept and the sense of tone are brought toward the I by three organisms. The organism of I can be added to the two described above. I-experience unfolds itself on all sides; it takes root on one side in a supersensible world equal in nature to itself, and enters into the organisms of concept and tone so that its own experience grows toward itself, as if it brought the organisms of I, of concept, and of tone to unfold like a blossom.

If we imagine the human being as a being of the sense world who incorporates a characteristic orientation, we are obliged to think of the polarity of up and down. "From above downward" is a direction in which we can think of the unfolding of the I-experience; "from below upward," the organism of I, toward which the I-experiences are growing, confronts this unfoldment. Just as leaves arrange themselves along the stem of a plant and unfold from below upward, so the formations of the organisms of concept and tone arrange themselves along the I-organism from above downward.

If it is now said—justifiably, after the above—that the primal I-experience unfolds out of a supersensible world, then it can be assumed that the forces at work in the formation of the organisms of I, concept, and tone possess the same substance that is present in the I-experience; however, these forces form this substance into structures that must already be present when the I-experience is perceived within sense perception. We can therefore conclude without much ado that the human I-experience is such that it flows out of a supersensible world—but can only be perceived when it takes root in an organism that itself is a composition of the organisms of I, concept, and tone; we could also say, in an organism that unfolds its sense organs within these three.

In addition, let us consider the astral body as it was described earlier. Its existence is indicated by image sensation, desire, and impulses for movement of the astral human being. Now it can easily be seen that, present within the organism of the I, is an image sensation that did not come about through a sense experience. The organism of the I is, after all, precisely the I-experience encountering itself from the opposite direction. Within the organism of concept we can recognize forces that unfold toward the inner human being—within the astral human being—as desire. A precise self-reflection will easily recognize the desire of the organism of concept in this organism's attraction for newly converging concepts. This is equally true for the organism of tone. It develops this desire for new meanings. In this, the activity of the astral body in bringing about the organisms of I, concept, and tone can be recognized.

An entity that would observe the I from outside, rather than experiencing it from within, as human beings do, could trace the coming about of the organism of I, and of the organisms of tone and concept. Such an entity would have to perceive the I-experience itself in such a way that it lets nothing of this I-experience enter but, rather, advances up to its boundary and, at this boundary, rays back the immanence of the I into itself. It is apparent that this process is the inverse of the so-called sense of touch. In the latter, the outer world is contacted and nothing of its nature is assimilated. The behavior of the presumed entity[1] toward the I is similar. However, with the sense of touch, the I enkindles only its own experiences through the contact and, thereby, experiences only its own content, whereas the presumed entity presses its own content into the I-experiences such that, within the I-experiences, this turns into a perception of the I. Thus when the I perceives itself, this occurs as a result of its [the presumed entity's] activity, which is of identical content with its experience of itself and differs from this

---

1. In chapter seven, *das angenommene äußere Wesen* has been consistently termed "the presumed outer entity." *Das Wesen* and *die Wesenhaftigkeit des Ich* has sometimes been translated as "the immanence of the I." — Trans.

only in that the activity shows it its own immanence from outside, whereas the I can experience this immanence only within itself.

In the case of the sense of concept, this presumed entity, when it comes into contact with the I, would have not only to ray back the experiences of concept, but also to impel them back into the I-experience, where they would then form the configuration of the organism of concept. It would not have to add anything to these experiences of concept, but only to maintain them within the process of experiencing concepts.

In the case of the organism of tone, however, maintaining would not be enough. Something needs to join the concept if it is to become tone. The hypothetical entity would have to transmit some of its own content into the I-experience.

A review of these relationships shows that, in the organism of I, only the I's individual immanence is rayed back from outside, while within the organism of concept the differently molded individual I-experience lets itself be directed back upon itself by something outward. Within the organism of tone, something of the very being of the outwardness then pours itself into the I-experience.

The presumed outer entity would have to perceive the coming about of the organism of I as an inverted experience of touch. It would have to sense the forming of the organism of concept in the way human beings experience their own life processes by means of the sense of life; the only difference would be that, in the case of the sense of

life, an inner configuration is being sensed, while the presumed entity would have to sense in its corresponding
sense how it molds itself into the I-experience of the
human being. Then, in the sense of tone, something pours
in from outside. If the presumed outer entity were to
experience this, it would have to occur through an
inverted sense of self-movement. Through it human
beings perceive their own movement; through its inversion, this entity would sense how its own being moves
inward into the I-experience. It would experience *itself* in
the I-being's carrying out an outer movement.

Now, in the human being the sense of life must be
founded in the life processes of the particular individual.
These life processes can be differentiated into the processes of breathing, warming, nourishing, secreting,
maintaining, growing, and generating, as has been
shown. The process of forming the organism of concept
can now indeed be imagined as a generating oriented
from without to within, and the forming of the organism
of tone as a part of the presumed outer entity growing
into the I-experience. We must, however, imagine that
the I-experiences themselves are used as substance of
this generating and growing.

By enlarging its scope, we can also apply the chosen
perspective to the other sense experiences and, thereby,
interpret these experiences with respect to what stands
behind them. In the case of the sense of hearing, our experience is that the sound points to an external object, while
the organ of hearing itself points to an activity that forms
it in a way similar to the way in which the organism of

concept is formed by the inverted sense of life and the tone organism by the inverted sense of self-movement. Let us now imagine that the sense of balance manifests itself in its inversion. Instead of maintaining uprightness when encountering the three outer directions of space as the sense of balance does in the human being, the inverted sense of balance would generate, within another entity, opposition to the three directions of space. If the above presumed entity were to indeed relate to the human being in such a way as to pour its own nature into the human being and, within the human being, bring about an opposition to the three directions of space, then the effect could be that the entity, which poured into the interior of the human I-experience, will be sensed as inner experience, while the activity of the inverted sense of balance would not be sensed, but would work in a way similar to the force that forms the organism of concept in the inverted sense of life, and the tone organism in the inverted sense of self-movement. The inverted sense of balance would then generate organ formation within the hearing organization.

Thus, sound points to the inwardness of something outward pouring across into the I-experience, whereas the organ of hearing points to an inverted sense of balance that has accumulated, and organically incorporated, the formations of the human being's immanence—similar to the inverted sense of life accumulating and combining experiences of concept. If the presumed outer entity is then, by its nature, actually assumed to be sound permeated by the inverted sense of balance, then it can also be imagined that the coming about of the hearing organization is founded in a process that enables the organ—while the outer entity comes into contact with the human being—to perceive the specific content of this outer entity, which flows toward the I-experience as sound, while the inverted sense of balance constitutes the activity underlying the sound, having molded the hearing organization out of the organism toward the experience of sound.[2]

How to interpret the sense of warmth becomes evident when the inversion of the sense of smell is reflected upon. In the sense of smell, external substance approaches the human being, and the experience of smell is a direct interaction with the substance. Its inversion would occur if the presumed outer entity were to consist of the content of the sensation of warmth, but permeated with an activity that enters into a direct interaction with the human being. Behind the content of the sensation of warmth would then stand an activity shaping the warmth organization. This activity would be such that warmth streams out from it, as smell streams out of an odorous substance. Just as smell spreads out into the outer world in all directions, this activity can be imagined as diverging out of the human being in all directions, unfolding in this divergence the organ-forming force for the sense of warmth. And just as outer substance discloses itself to the sense of smell, the human interior would have to disclose itself to this activity. Such a disclosure would happen if

---

2. For an alternate version of this last paragraph, see page 144.

the outward-striving activity were underlain by a kind of life process, which is to say, if this activity were to saturate the human being with its own nature. The sense of warmth would thereby be based on a kind of nourishing of the human being with the substance that discloses itself, in terms of its content, in the sense experience of warmth.

For an interpretation of the sense of sight, the inversion of the experience of taste should be considered. If the organ of seeing were to come about through an outer activity of a being such as the hypothetical entity assumed above—in such a way, for example, that color would saturate this entity while being completely permeated by an activity that an inverted tasting represents—then this taste-radiating activity could be considered an organ-forming force of the sense of sight. Unlike the effect of an outer substance that we experience as taste, the situation here would have to be such that this being would radiate taste toward itself, from within the human being. Just as the human being brings about a change in the substance in the case of taste, so this outer entity would have to undertake a change in the human interior. Such a change, however, is present in inner life processes—in the process of warming, for example. Warming in the human being would have to result from the taste radiating from within outward. However, this warming would not proceed like an outer warmth process because its substance is not outer warmth but something identical in content to the sense experience of sight. We see that in *this* warming, occurring through the activity that radiates outward from within the human being and founded in the color of the presumed entity, there lies the inner nature of light itself. Not the experience of sight, but, lying behind this experience of sight, the *inner* nature of light kindles a warming that lives in the organ-forming force of the sense of sight, just as the substance, interacting with the sense of taste, lives in the experience of taste.

The sense of taste can also be characterized as an inverted sense of smell. However, in that case the inversion has a different meaning than it does in the comparison between the senses of taste and sight. Let us suppose that, in the organ of smell, an inversion were to take place such that a smell is not sent from a substance into the human interior, but instead the inversion makes the smell rebound upon contact. Then we would indeed be given an analogue to the human organ of taste. The human interior, however, would itself have to be put in the place of the above presumed outer entity. But while that hypothetical entity lets its nature approach the human being from the outside, its counterpart with regard to the sense of smell would have to be enclosed in the human being. To the extent that the human organism activates the sense of smell, it is filled with something external or foreign to its essence. Something outer has become interiorized and, from within, unfolds forces like those that were active in forming the organs of sight, hearing, and warmth.

It is reasonable that in the sense of smell something comes to expression that can be equated with an inner immanence of outwardness. And, if the sense of taste is the inversion of this, it is justified to say: what hits the human being as disclosure from outside in the experience of taste is the same as what acts within in the organ of smell. But then, between the sense of taste and the sense of smell, there must be a point where the outer world and the inner world show themselves to be the same. And we may imagine that something stands behind the experience of smell, which—as *substance* of the outer world within the interior of the human being—is truly active in the molding of organs, particularly in the build-up of the organ of taste. This, then, is built up by the *substance* of the outer world.

Within the organ of smell, only the outward-streaming substance that perceives itself directly in the experience of smell must then be imagined. The sensation of smell, then, would thus be self-perception of substance, and the organ of taste would be the self-enlivening of substance.

These considerations were meant to point out that, behind sense experience, nothing more concerning substance needs to be imagined, but rather only spiritual immanence. The sense experiences would then be revelations of the spiritual. To sense observation, sense experience directly reveals itself, but not the spiritual lying behind it.

. . . . .

Alternate version of paragraph beginning on page 139:

Thus, sound points to the inwardness of something outward, pouring across into the I-experience, while the organ of hearing points to an inverted experience of balance that accumulates and organically combines the formations of the human being's immanence, similar to the inverted sense of life accumulating and combining experiences of concept. If the presumed outer entity is then, by its nature, actually assumed to be sound permeated by the inverted sense of balance, then it can also be reasoned that the coming about of the hearing organization is based on an immanence of being in the outer world that is given in the sense experience of the sense of balance, if the sense of balance is thought of as inverted—that is, not imagined as directed into the human being, but as raying outward.

CHAPTER 8

THE WORLD UNDERLYING
THE ORGANS OF LIFE

The consideration of the I's experience in the organism of I-concept and in the organisms of concept and tone resulted in an image similar to that of a plant form unfolding from above downward. The remainder of the human being in its entirety can likewise be imagined as what confronts the I-experience from below upward, constraining the downward stream of the I-experience and, to a degree, holding it at bay within itself. In this remainder the being is found that enters existence through birth. This being is the temporal precondition of what strives—in the image above—from above downward. We can thus say that what works from below upward to confront the I-experience appears on Earth at birth. What was earlier described as the activities forming the sense organs must, therefore, already have taken place within this human being. In that case the forming of these sense organs can only be imagined such that the organ-forming forces bore themselves as streams into the human, striving from below upward. Here, the image of forces converging inward from different sides comes to mind. These forces encircle the human being, and they must also experience a constraint like that encountered by the I-experience streaming downward from above in the entire human being striving upward from below.

What this constraint is becomes clear when we think of the forces that form the sense organs encountering those forces present in the life processes. If we think of the inverted sense of balance working counter to the activity of the force of sound, we have the disposition for the organ of hearing. If we imagine the inverted sense of smell working counter to the force of the warmth experience, we have the disposition for the organ of warmth. The organ of warmth is spread out over the entire human being. This fact fits into the picture formed by letting the inverted sense of taste run in the opposite direction from the inverted senses of smell and balance. The inverted sense of smell then runs through the entire body, and the inverted sense of taste runs from the other side, which, together with the force of the experience of light, shows itself active in molding the organ for the sense of sight. Within the sense of taste itself, the substance that is active in molding its organ discloses itself in the sense of smell. It finds itself constrained by the organism that was built up by the remaining senses. In the sense of smell, inwardness of substance works toward the inwardness of substance. Here we come to the image of a peripheral circle from which the organ-molding forces proceed, working on the human being, as it were, at the circle's center. If these were the *only* organ-molding forces, a totally different configuration and order of the sense organs would result than is the case in reality.

What arises in reality can, however, only occur if the organ-molding forces are constrained as they unfold.

Suppose that the organ-molding force for the latent organ of hearing is strengthened in one place and diminished in another; it will then make itself especially noticeable in one place. This is precisely what happens when other forces work on the organ-molding forces themselves. The question then arises as to whether anything in the human being points to the existence of such forces outside us. To begin with, the life processes show something special. They carry on even when, during sleep, sensory experiences are at rest. This shows that formative forces must be at work in their organs even when the senses are turned off. So the forces that shape the sense organs are, in a way, only one side of organ-molding activity. Before the life processes can be present, they must be prepared by the organ-molding forces of the life organs.

Now, the forces in which the organs of life are grounded are even further removed from human consciousness than the ones that build up the sense organs. In the sense organs, forces show their effects that reveal themselves through the sense organs. However, the forces that build up the organs of life are not revealed in these organs, but only their effects— that is, the organs themselves. By means of the organ of warmth, we sense warmth; by means of the sense of life, we sense the organs of life. The coming about of the life organs thus presupposes the existence of a different world than does the forming of the sense organs. However, the sense organs do have to integrate harmoniously with the life organs. Thus, for sense organs to come about in their appropriate shape, the disposition for the senses must already be present in the forces that build up the life organs. This, however, points to the existence of a world in which the formative forces of the life organs work in such a way as to predispose the sense organs within the life organs without, however, forming the sense organs themselves. Only after the life organs have been formed do these forces imprint the sense organs into the form of these life organs.

Now, not all sense organs need to be present already in the same way in the organ-forming forces of the life organs. The organs of the so-called sense of touch do not need to be present at all, since they only reflect the experiences of the life organs back into themselves. From the senses of life, self-movement, and balance, what has significance only when the sense organs are imprinted on the life organs, may be absent as well. Thus, that which is related to the feeling-like experiences of the senses of life and self-movement with regard to the sense organs themselves is not present in these dispositions. With this, however, we have pointed to a world in which is found the organ-molding forces of the life organs and the *dispositions* for the organ-molding forces for the senses of hearing, warmth, sight, taste, and smell.

If the sense organs now imprint themselves on pre-existing life organs, the formative forces of the life organs must have created a foundation within the life organs. On this foundation, the life organs develop the life processes, and into the life processes the organ-molding forces of the senses pour their currents. These organ-molding forces thus experience a constraint in the life organs. Their activity impacts against this constraint. The senses can be developed only in places where the life organs permit this to happen. The very image of the human being shows that the polarity of left-right and right-left is worth considering with regard to the distribution of the sense organs we have mentioned. The bilateral symmetry in the structure of the human being shows that the life organs and sense organs relate in two different ways. If we look at the sense organs in a person who is facing us, we can see that the right ear, for example, inasmuch as it owes its origin to the stage in which the forces that mold the organs of life prevail, has been shaped from left to right, and that it has then become a sense organ, because the forces molding the sense organs confront the just described forming process from right to left. The reverse would hold true for the left ear. Something similar would apply to the other symmetrically distributed sense organs.

Inasmuch as we are beings who experience by means of sense organs, our origin can be sought in the world described earlier as the world from which the astral human being stems. If we also consider that the forces molding the sense organs are the inversions of sense experiences themselves, we may assume that we are talking about the world out of which the astral human being stems, when we presuppose an entity that shapes our sense organs through forces impacting as it were from outside. This is because it has shown itself that inverted sense experiences flow into the human being when the sense organs are molded. Thus image sensations are roused through these forces. But image sensations, in addition to desire and impulses for movement, point to the astral body of the human being. If we also now imagine the forces that mold the sense organs as inversions of movement impulses and desires, we have an idea of how the human astral body, as shaper of the sense organs, hails from a world that is imperceptible to the senses.

A realm where the world of sense experience is grounded is thus assumed, which has been called the "astral world." We must then take everything we experience sense-perceptibly as immediate reality and presuppose the existence of an astral world concealing itself within. The former is called the *physical world*. It is grounded in the *astral world*. We have now seen that the astral world is grounded in yet another world. The organ-molding forces of the life organs, and the disposition for the senses of hearing, warmth, sight, and taste, are rooted in that other world. Since that world contains the formative forces for the life organs, we can say that human beings themselves—inasmuch as the formative forces for the life organs are present in their bodies—also originate in that world. If we call the sum total of the forces that shape the life organs in the human being (in the sense of page 147) the human "etheric body," then we can recognize that this *etheric body* has its origin in the world lying beyond the astral world. This world has been called the "lower spiritual world," by which, again, nothing more is meant than what has been asserted here.[1]

Among the life processes are now three processes whose organs point to a world above and beyond the one

---

1. See, for example, Rudolf Steiner's *At the Gates of Spiritual Science* and *The Theosophy of the Rosicrucian*, where "lower spiritual world" is also called "lower devachan." — ED.

in which, in accordance with the above, the origin of the life organs is to be sought. In *generating*, the living physical body repeats its own formation; in *growth*, it augments what subsists with something new, made out of the substance of what subsists; in *maintaining*, what subsists acts on what subsists; and in *secreting*, something that the life process contains is excreted from it. These are, therefore, life processes that take place within the organs of life. This is not the case in nourishing, warming, and breathing. These processes are possible only when the life organs take up something from a world external to themselves.

Among the sense experiences are five whose organs similarly point beyond the world where the origin of the organs corresponding to the other sensory experiences is to be sought. According to what was described earlier, the sense of taste is an inverted sense of smell, inasmuch as the sense of taste turns inward the experience that, through the sense of smell, was sensed on contact with outer substance, so that the smell of the substance already located within the body is tasted. The sense of taste therefore presupposes a substance already located within the organism. The organ of smell, however, presupposes the substance of the outer world. For the sense of sight, we can conclude, from what we have considered above, that its organ comes about when an entity is active in this inception who does not treat color experiences in the way that occurs when they are sensed through the sense of sight, but rather shifts them into an activity that is contrary to the one from which the organ of taste is built-up. When such an activity is latent in an organism, an organ of sight can thus come about through a transformation of a latent organ of taste into an organ of sight. Whereas an organ of smell is inconceivable without contact with an outer substance, and an organ of taste is an organ of smell turned inward, thus presupposing a substance located within, the organ of sight can come about when an organ of taste, latently present, is not developed to its completion, but transformed within. Substance must then pour toward this organ along an inner path. It is the same with the organ of warmth. It can be seen as an organ of smell whose formation has ben arrested and transfigured for the same reason given for the sense of sight. (The organ of taste is thus seen as an organ of smell that has simply been *inverted*—that is, turned inside out—while the organ of warmth is to be seen as a *transformed* organ of smell.) In the same way, the organ of hearing would result from a transformed organ of balance; the organ for tone as an organ of self-movement that has been arrested prematurely in its formation; and the organ for concept as an organ of the sense of life that has been transformed right in its inception. The formation of these organs therefore presupposes no external substance, but it suffices that the substance streaming within is taken hold of by higher formative forces than those prevailing in the sense of smell.

For the organ of smell, on the other hand, contact with external substance is necessary. Now the sense of balance does presuppose contact with outer substance, but it does presuppose a relationship to the three directions of space. If these directions existed in empty space, there could be no sense of balance—it can exist only when space is permeated by substance and when the permeation by substance is pervaded by forces, to which the human body brings itself into relationship. But if an interrelationship is to come about, forces must relate to other forces. Thus, the human body must counter within itself the three forces of space-permeating substance with three forces in its own substance. The human body must therefore possess an organ that not only relates to outer substance, as does the organ of smell, but through which its three directions of force can be sensed.

Now, we have shown above that the inverted sense of balance can be thought of as being active in formative development of the organ of hearing. Let us now suppose that this inverted sense of balance were to develop an existing disposition for hearing to a stage beyond the formative development of an organ of hearing—that is, the formative development is not completed in the moment when an organ of hearing is formed, but goes on developing from there. The disposition for hearing would then turn into an organ of balance. In the same way, it can now be imagined that the inverted sense of self-movement would develop a disposition for the organ of tone, beyond the inherent nature of the disposition for tone. Through a corresponding organ, the human being would not perceive tone, but would sense the relationship that exists to forces of outer substance. And if the inverted sense of life were to develop an organ of concept far beyond its formative development, it would sense the relationship of its own substance to outer substance through a resulting organ. For this to be possible, not only would the substance have to prove operative within the human body, but it would have to be able, from the outside, to let its forces play into the human body, without touching the body. We would then find in the senses of balance, self-movement, and life three organs that would require the outer world in order to come about. For the sense of touch, this is clear from the very beginning, since it recognizes an outer world only through a concealed judgment, therefore definitively presupposing an outer world.

Thus we can say that the organs of taste, sight, warmth, and hearing are organs which can be formed in an organism through the forces of substance streaming around *within it*; for the senses of smell, balance, self-movement, life, and touch, outer substance together with its forces proves to be a prerequisite.

Just as the life organs point to the outer world of substance in breathing, warming, and nourishing, so do the organs of the senses mentioned above. On the other hand, secreting, maintaining, growing, and generating, and the organisms of taste, sight, and hearing, tone, concept and I presuppose inner formative principles that can only work on interiorized substance.

CHAPTER 9

THE HIGHER
SPIRITUAL WORLD

If it is now supposed, as we have done above, that the formative forces for the life organs and the dispositions for the forces of the sense organs lie in the lower spiritual world, then, for the forming forces within this world, a natural distinction appears between those forces that presuppose an interiorized substance and those forces that form their organs to receive substance from outside. It is easily seen that the latter are a prerequisite of the former, since, if substance had no inherent possibility for interiorization, it could not become effective within itself. Therefore, the forces at work within substance must be forces that allow it to call up countereffects from what is external to itself. Indeed, the content of the previous chapter points to such countereffects of substance upon itself. The inverted senses of life, self-movement, and balance carry within themselves the concealed possibility of their becoming active, as substance itself, to call forth interior formative development, but without making use of inner formative principles as such. They are active *outside*, not just *within,* the scope of these formative principles. If we now imagine these three inverted sensory activities acting in a way that does not impinge on an inwardly molded organ, while still remaining within the inherent nature of their sphere of effectiveness, they arrive at a limit where they must return back into themselves. At this limit, substance would throw itself back into itself; it would constrain itself in itself. What is present at this limit could be called substantiality within substantiality.

This would point to the possibility that those organs requiring inner substance come about out of a world in which substance outside becomes substance inside. This world would have to include the first dispositions for both those life organs that are supplied with interiorized substance and those that require outer substance. Within those forces that interiorize outer substance, this interiorization would have to be already present. Just as the forces in the life organs themselves point to a world of other forces out of which the life organs are shaped to begin with, the life organs with substance streaming within them point to dispositions in a still higher world out of which they are formed. We are thus led to point to an exterior world that can engender an exterior world through the antipode of the senses of life, self-movement, and balance. This world can be called the "higher spiritual world."

What could be looked for in this world? Not forces that ultimately shape the life organs, but those that implant the disposition to become life organs into their configurations. We must imagine these forces, however, as the antipodes of the senses of balance, self-movement, and life. If these forces are held back before they reach the limit of their sphere of effectiveness by inner formative processes in organs already in the process of being formed, they fashion the organs for the senses of hearing, tone, and concept out of these latent organs. What happens when these forces reach the limit of their natural, inherent activity? If the inverted sense of life were not to encounter anything to transform in the organ of concept, then it would obviously lead the experience of concept back into itself. And it would encounter itself directly as it rays back. This would then be the same process that is present in a sense experience, but it would lead an independent existence, without being based on an underlying sense organ. Something similar could be said of the inverted senses of self-movement and balance. In the higher spiritual world we would thus have to look for sensory experiences that are sufficient unto themselves. They are related to the sensory experiences closest to the human being's I in the physical world—namely, the experiences of the senses of concept, tone, and hearing. In the case of these higher experiences, however, it is not, as it were, as if there were a human I standing before them and taking them in. Rather, it is as if a being were standing behind them, creating them in its own activity.

CHAPTER 10

THE HUMAN FORM

Based on the above considerations, we can state the following formative principles with regard to the human being.

We are presupposing:

1. *A higher spiritual world*; in it lie forces that shape the configurations that constitute sense experiences within self-determined substance. Impressed into these configurations are the dispositions for the life organs.

2. A *lower spiritual world*; in it lie the formative forces of the life organs. The forces active in the higher spiritual world shape those configurations molded by previously interiorized substance. The forces of the lower spiritual world join to these configurations those that first interiorize outer substance. This differentiates the life organs into organs that generate and organs that nourish. The configurations shaped by the higher spiritual world are transformed into dispositions for sense organs that are nourished by interiorized substance. The formative forces of the lower spiritual world join to

these dispositions for senses those that interact with outer substance.

3. *The astral world*; in it lie the formative forces of the sense organs. However, the life organs must also be shaped out of this world in such a way that they can incorporate the sense organs into themselves.

4. *The physical world*; in it lie the sense experiences of the human being.

We must now recognize that these four worlds work into each other, that the forces of each higher one persist in the lower one. Since the organs we have named derive from the forces of higher worlds, we can say only that these organs are subject to the influences of higher worlds even when they appear in the lower worlds. The higher worlds' forces do not work from the physical world upon the sense organs; the two spiritual worlds' forces do not work from the astral world upon the life organs; and the higher spiritual world's forces do not work from the lower spiritual upon the disposition for the life forces characterized above. From this it follows that, out of the physical world, the forces of the higher worlds must show themselves to be effective in a different way than they do when they are working directly out of their own world. The forces of the higher spiritual world can affect the human being, who is endowed with sense organs, life organs, and organ dispositions, only as formative forces. They can determine the form and location of the organs. Thus, the form and location of the human body's organs result from the effect of the higher spiritual world as it works into the physical world.

In the perception of concept, the I *experiences* concepts; the inverted form of the sense of life *generates* the living concepts of the higher spiritual world. Within the physical world, these living concepts can act only as formative forces. Clearly, the human being owes the ability to perceive concepts to upright posture. Apart from the human being, no being on Earth has perception of concept, none the same kind of upright posture. (A simple reflection can show that an apparently upright posture in animals is due to something other than inner forces.) Thus, the direction from below upward can be seen as the direction that relates to the perception of concept when the inverted sense of life is not involved in the process. From this we may conclude that a direction from above downward applies to the inverted sense of life. It would be more accurate to say, "a direction *approximating* from above downward." This is because, in the direction of growth from below upward, something should be seen that is antipodal to the inverted sense of touch. Inasmuch as, in the sense of the earlier exposition, the I constitutes an antipode to the sense of touch, the vertical direction of the body's growth upward as bearer of the I can be seen as a continual overcoming of downward-bearing weight, where the latter indeed constitutes an inversion of the experience of touch.

From all this, a polarity can be pointed to in the human body, between "above-downward" and "below-upward," as if a current were streaming from below upward in such a way that the inverted sense of life, working from above downward, is overcome.[1] Now in this inverted sense of life, the higher spiritual world working into the physical human body must be seen. We can therefore say: the human body, inasmuch as it is the bearer of the I, strives upward; the physical human body, inasmuch as it shows the effects of the higher spiritual world in its form, strives from above downward. Insofar as the bodily aspect of the human being expresses the image of an entity belonging to the higher spiritual world, the human being can be seen as the interpenetration of two directions of force, as the meeting of the I body and the physical body. In the experience of I, the human being belongs to the physical outer world, but at the same time constitutes an image of this experience raying back into itself. This is an image of what has been characterized as the sense experiences sufficient unto themselves in the higher spiritual world. Thus we may see the body, inasmuch as it is the bearer of the I, as an *image* of substance interiorizing itself.

A different polarity appears in "back-to-front" and "front-to-back." The sense organs, together with the nerves belonging to them, constitute organs that essentially manifest their growth pattern from front-to-back; if they are imagined—as is certainly justified—growing in a way that their formative forces are antipodal to the original direction of growth stemming from the lower

---

1. The printed sheets corrected by Rudolf Steiner end here. The remaining text is taken from the manuscript.

spiritual world, then this original direction may be looked for in the direction from back-to-front. We can then say that the closure of the human form toward the back is similar, with regard to the lower spiritual world, to the closure from below upward, with regard to the higher spiritual world. Furthermore, with regard to the process of molding their outer shape, the life organs would be worked on from front-to-back by those forces of the lower spiritual world that cannot work on the human being out of the physical world; from back-to-front, however, the forces of the lower spiritual world would work into the physical human world. Within these latter forces is expressed what we may call, in the sense of our earlier considerations, the astral human being. Thus, inasmuch as the astral human being shows itself in its bodily manifestation, it strives from back-to-front in just the same way as the physical human body strives upward.

The third polarity would then be that of right-left and left-right. The symmetry of the human form with regard to this direction suggests that here the forces face each other in equal measure. We come to this result when we ascertain a concurrence, in these directions, of the human bodily form with the formative forces of the sense organs, insofar as the human bodily form has already formed the human bodily organs out of the lower spiritual world.[2] In the left half of the forward-facing body

---

2. This sentence reflects a probable typographical error in the German edition: *Leibesorgane* = "the bodily organs" rather than *Lebens-organe* = "life organs." — TRANS.

we would therefore have to imagine the formative forces of the astral world for the sense organs, insofar as these forces do not continue their action into the physical world, as working from the left half of the body toward the right; those forces of the astral world that do continue to work on the bodily form so that their effect manifests in the bodily form would have to work toward the left. Since these forces have to work on organs already determined out of the lower spiritual world, they will show themselves in an effect that is inwardly directed, as the forces of the higher and lower spiritual worlds show themselves in outwardly manifested formations. (Evidence for what has been said can be found referred to in anthropology as the pathways of the senses, which cross in the organism.)

This points to an interpenetration of the astral world with the human ether body, inasmuch as the latter comes to expression in the bodily form. We can therefore say:

1. The forming of the physical human body in the direction from above downward is determined out of the higher spiritual world.

2. The form of the human body, inasmuch as it is the bearer of the astral human being, points to the direction from back-to-front.

3. The form of the human body, inasmuch as it is the bearer of the life processes, points to the directions from right-left as well as left-right.

4. The result of these forming processes would then be the actual physical human form.

For this form to arise, however, the formative forces mentioned must interpenetrate. Such an interpenetration can only be imagined if the human being stands in the physical world so that the forces of the outer physical world are taken hold of along the right-left and left-right direction by the forces of the astral world—so that, in its formative development, the possibility remains open to continued formation in the direction of back-to-front and, after that, the direction from above downward. How this comes about can only be pictured when a direction is imagined that runs right-left and left-right in principle, is active toward all sides, and is then altered in the forward direction and transformed again when pulled upward.

For this to result in the human form, however, these forces must be imagined as antipodal to forces from the physical world, which are, however, *not operative out of* the physical world. These latter forces are operative directly out of the higher worlds, as we have character- ized above [but work all the way into the physical world]. Only the latter may be sought in the human physical dis- position. Only *as such a disposition* does the human being relate to the other forces.[3] If we thus seek indications of higher worlds from the human being within the physical world, we may not look to the life processes and how they relate to the corresponding organs, nor to the life of the sense organs, and also not to the brain, but solely to the *how*, to the form of the human figure and its organs. This

---

3. That is, those forces *not* working all the way into the physical world. — TRANS.

"how" can show that it is indeed possible to perceive indications of the spiritual worlds even in the physical human being. (The difference between human beings and animals with regard to the higher worlds can thus be derived from a consideration of their respective bodily forms, inasmuch as the animal is differently aligned to the directions of space. This different alignment shows, however, that the higher worlds work differently on animals than they do on human beings.)

Anthroposophical considerations can be made fruitful, when the above considerations are applied to the specifics of the human bodily form, and will prove to be in complete harmony with anthropological observations in each case. It has been indicated how the organs of hearing, sight, and so on, are latent organs transformed in the process of becoming, and how the organ of taste is an inverted organ of smell. Such indications can result in mental pictures that must be rediscovered in the forms of the organs. The asymmetrical organs are comprehended when it is understood that their shapes were molded in a way that made it possible to exclude the forces active in the "left-right" and "right-left" of the astral world.

Having acknowledged, as we have done above, an inversion or turning "outside-in" of the sense organs, it can be readily allowed that such a transformation can also be caused by other principles. Let us consider the organ of hearing. The organ of hearing has been brought into relationship to the sense of balance. It is conceivable that the activity manifesting itself in the sense of balance diverts a latent organ, not yet particularized as an organ of hearing, and directed inward, from its original direction of development. The sense of tone would arise if a different activity were to direct itself onto the corresponding latent organ. The latter could be brought into relationship to the experiences of the sense of self-movement. This sheds light on the fact that the organ of hearing comes to expression in an organ inclined toward outer substance, while the organ for the sense of tone cannot be outwardly perceptible. The experience of the sense of self-movement corresponds to the inside of the body, while the experience of the sense of balance comes to expression in relationships to the outer directions of space. Accordingly, we could also call the organ for the sense of tone an organ of hearing that has been held back within the body.

For the experience of the I itself, which does not correspond to any sense experience, no particular organ would come into consideration, but only the striving upward of the other latent organs. Thus we may recognize the organs of the senses of tone and concept as formations whose physical form is determined by their inclination toward the I-experience.

Within this, where the body as I-bearer participates from within, the inversion of the formative forces can be recognized, and it can be said that when the body as I-bearer regresses the formation of an organ, the signature of the configurations of the higher spiritual world must be recognizable in the *image* of this organ. One such organ is that of speech (the larynx). If the sequence of organs of the ear, the sense of tone, and the sense of concept can be seen as a continual bodily interiorization of the disposition for sense, then the organ of speech can be recognized as the inversion of the sense of tone. In this case the tone does not become a sense experience that strives inward toward the I by way of an organ, but is creative sensory content at rest in itself, a truly inverted sense experience. The formative development of the larynx corresponds exactly to these conditions.

We can then also look for an organ that corresponds to a capability in the human being that lies between speaking and I, just as comprehension lies between hearing and I. Through this organ, something would have to arise out of the human being that is not as meager in content as the I-experience, and whose manifestations do not yet flow over directly into the outer world. This would be the organ in the human brain that corresponds to imagination or fantasy.[4] We will gradually learn to distinguish between the organ of concept and the organ of fantasy in the brain.

Since the forming forces of the three higher worlds, in some sense, resound in the form of the physical human body, we must also recognize that the formative forces of the two higher spiritual worlds are able to work directly onto the astral body out of the astral world; and, finally, that effects stream directly from the higher spiritual world into the dispositions for life organs, as they are present in the lower spiritual world. The form and location of the

---

4. The German word *Phantasie* can have either of these meanings, that is "fantasy" or "imagination." — TRANS.

heart, the organs of respiration and circulation, the systems of muscles and bones, and so on, can result when such forces are taken into account.

The form of the human body within the physical world shows that its development did not simply result from an adaptation to conditions foreign to the inner human being. This form, rather, ultimately expresses, in image form, what is characteristic of the I. The disposition for development of the human being must be imagined as offering points of contact for the forces of the higher spiritual worlds when specific forms develop out of the disposition.

In the sense-perceptible world, *only* contents of sensation are present for perception, contents that the I confronts as image sensation when it perceives itself. Image sensation, however, belongs to the astral world. In the I's experience of itself, therefore, image sensation hovers, as it were, freely in space.

It is possible, as we have seen, to recognize an inverted sense of smell in the sense of taste. If, instead of thinking that the sensation of smell is caused by the impacting substance, we think of the experience of smell itself as self-experience in the I that becomes a component of the I, then we can see the astral I's desire or impulse for movement as this I's response to something that proceeds from substance and is incorporated into the I, without physical mediation. In addition to the image experience behind the experience of smell, then, there is also an astral response to the desires and movement impulses of the I.

In the case of sound, we can clearly distinguish between what frees itself from the external object and what is perceived of the object by senses other than the sense of hearing. And what has freed itself is self-experience of the I. We can certainly say that when an object is heard, only the vibrating object belongs to the world in which the I is not included and unable to identify itself with the sense experience.

In the sense of self-movement, the position and change in form of our own organism is perceived. Here, then, it is not far-fetched to think that, in addition to the I's self-experience, only an astral countereffect to an impulse for movement needs to be assumed.

If, now, nothing but sense experiences are present in the physical world, then *within* this world only sense experiences can be spoken of. However, since a physical body must have sense organs to be able to have sense experiences, for the human being in this physical world, nothing exists but sense experiences and the perception of I as astral image experience. The I has no other possibility than to experience objects of the outer world and thereby to find sense experiences combined in manifold ways. What happens in this case, then, is nothing but sense experiences hovering freely in space.

Let us, however, assume that the human form as such is not without meaning but that the orientation and position of one organ in relation to another is significant. Let us consider the physical world from this point of view. Then it is significant that the organ of taste is an inverted organ of smell. This is because of the following: Let us imagine the experience of smell, as it appears as image sensation. In so doing, however, let us not deny the capacity of space-filling substance to present this experience as image sensation, in the same way that the I-perception is image sensation hovering freely in space. Then we must acknowledge that it is of significance which part of the surface of the human form is oriented toward an object; to receive the image sensation emanating from the object, sometimes this and sometimes that sense organ must be oriented toward it. For the human being in the physical world, however, it can only be concluded that the human being perceives a smell in one instance, a taste in another, depending on the organ used. If, however, the I were to encompass not only I-perception in the physical world, but were to underlie the bodily form in such a way that it experienced all image experiences as its own, the image sensation present in this I, the image sensation of smell in one instance, that of taste at another would be self-experience of the I. If we were dealing not with the finished, but with the bodily form in development, no I-perception would be present; the self-experience of the I would have to be totally different.

APPENDIX 1

An earlier version of text beginning with "We are present with our I..." page 100, in Chapter 3.

The text below can be assumed to be the first version of the contents beginning on page 100. These contents, however, were rewritten by Rudolf Steiner in the form in which they then appeared in his final manuscript and in the corrected printed sheets. The sentence "We are present with our I..." (page 100) and the words "We are totally justified..." (page 101) are the same in both versions, but the content of what follows them is different.

... We are present with our I in everything there is to experience in the sense world, and our soul world develops within the I on the basis of sensory experiences. We are not present at the building up of our sensory organism. Reflection, however, will tell us that existence cannot stop at what we perceive with our senses, because without an existence that is imperceptible to the senses, we could have no senses to use for sensory perception.

We are totally justified, in contrast to the human being who is evident in the sense world, in speaking of another human being who cannot be revealed in this world. The first interacts with the sense-perceptible world and, out of it, develops a soul life; the second interacts with a different world and develops, out of it, the capacities for sense perception. The second human being is contained, as it were, within the first. But the second makes up a much finer configuration therein than the first. Soul life, as it develops on the basis of the world of sense perception, reveals itself in the outer form of the human being's configuration. Just consider the face of someone on whom the sun of life has always smiled, and see how different it is from one on which life's heavy sorrows have left significant traces. If we continue to reflect along these lines, we will soon arrive at ideas of how in the physiognomy, in the expression, in the gesture, and even in the form of the person's body, the character of the soul life is revealed. Within limits, this is also a result of the interrelationship between the human being and the sense-perceptible outer world. However, this revelation has something unspecific about it; it is constantly shifting and evolving. It does not offer a stable configuration. On the other hand, the capacity to have sense perceptions as such is, to a great extent, something finished and solid, forming a basis on which we actually build up our mobile, conscious soul life.

Just as it is not far-fetched to differentiate between the outer world and the inner human soul world—through their interrelationship, the latter appears as a reflection of the former—so it is not far-fetched to assume a comparable difference between a hidden outer world and a human inner world that lies concealed behind the one in which the I lives when basing itself on the sense-perceptible world alone. We can distinguish between the world that lies spread out before the human being—when one or more of the gates of the senses is open—and what is within the human being but connected to that world by means of the interrelationship between them. Here we will apply the term "sense world" to what is in the world spread out in this way. What we encounter within the human being, as just described, will be called the "I-human being." For the moment, let us not associate anything with this name other than its immediate usage here.

The world out of which the capacity for sense perception is formed—in a similar way, for example, to how mental pictures are formed out of the sense world—will be called the "etheric world"; and what is born in the human being out of this etheric world, just as the I-being is born out of the sense world, will be called the "astral being." In using the term "etheric world" we should not think of the "ether" of physics, nor should we think of anything other than what has just been characterized here in using the term "astral being." In this way, an etheric world underlies the sense world just as an astral being underlies the I-being. Just as the etheric world cannot be sense-perceptible because it is what generates the senses in the first place, so the astral being also cannot be experienced with the senses because it must precede the development of sensory capacities.

. . . . .

We can now tackle looking at the human being from yet another side. To begin with, the human being appears as a being within the sense world. This appearance, however, is subject to change. In different ages of life, the particularities of the human being are different. When we look at a child as a sense-perceptible being, we can in no way see from what the senses present what it will develop into in adulthood. And yet we must assume that the circumstances, the forces, that will cause the adult to emerge from the child are already present. Here, too, an exact reflection shows that existence, or what is real, conceals within itself more than is perceptible in the sense world.

Describing the process of growth provides contemplation with an opportunity to gain an idea of what is concealed here. Until the second dentition around the seventh year, the activity of what is concealed works primarily at configuring the outer human being. Around this time, the organs of the outer body have assumed their lasting configurations. From then on, although the limbs continue to grow, the configurations that have been established are never actually reshaped. From then on, the concealed inwardness begins a life within itself, and opens itself up to the forces that unfold their activity more in this inwardness. In the first years of life, the inner forces strive toward the outer body as formative forces; in the following years, they remain more inwardly predisposed, until they are mature enough to transpose their nature onto another being—that is, until the individual becomes capable of reproduction. We must recognize what develops within the human being, imperceptible to the senses, to the point of sexual maturity, as what can be transmitted to one's descendants.

At this point we must consider something that is important for our understanding of the nature of the human being. The conditions for what can be transmitted to one's physical descendants lie in something that achieves a certain completion in its development when sexual maturity is reached. If anything of what the human being acquires at a later stage in life is to be passed on, it must first be incorporated into the forces that are already present at sexual maturity. It can be passed on only indirectly, through these forces. Once sexual maturity is achieved, of course, all the essential conditions for heredity must already be developed.

At sexual maturity, what transmits itself from inside to outside ceases to develop in the human being. In the early stages of childhood, it reveals itself as the forces shaping the body; later, it works inwardly in such a way that the human being can pass on configurations to descendants. If human development continues beyond this stage, it can only take place inwardly. What continues to develop must primarily be experienced as inner content, as soul content. This, however, may not be equated with that conscious content of soul that is lit up by the I and develops out of sensory perception. There is a certain inner development that is not in the hands of the I in the same way as the development of conscious soul content. Coming to meet the soul life that is stimulated from outside through sensory perception is not the same as what comes from inside and causes each individual to take in the sense-perceptible outer world with a very particular nuance of soul. That is, there is something within the human being that comes to meet sensory stimuli, something that does not yet belong to the human domain of being stimulated by the senses. Through simple reflection, so to speak, we come to an "inner human being" concealed behind the I-human being, because it must already be present before the I-human being's life can begin.

It is not difficult to recognize that this inner human being is the same as the one we have described as interacting with a hidden world behind the sense world. This inner being cannot have been evoked by those inner forces whose development is concluded at sexual maturity, since it continues to develop thereafter. It cannot be attributed to the human being who expresses him or herself in giving shape to the body and in transmitting its nature to descendants. Instead, it must be rooted in an entity that has nothing to do with the manifestation of human forces that we have just mentioned. It also cannot originate in the same way as these force-manifestations, for these cause human beings to reveal outwardly what they carry within themselves. However, this inner being must actually interrelate with what is outward, because it continues to develop even when the inner shaping forces and hereditary conditions have reached completion. Everything about this inner human being justifies our equating it with what we called the "astral human being" earlier on.

We would therefore have to presuppose effects in the etheric world whose significance for this astral being is similar to that of sense impressions for the I-being. The astral being takes shape out of the etheric world in the same way that the I-being does out of the sense world. Behind all of the sense world, therefore, an interaction takes place between an etheric world and an astral human being. To use an image once again, we have here an expanse of ocean, imperceptible to the senses, in which an interaction is taking place between the etheric world and the astral being; the interplay between the sense world and the I-being rises like dry land out of this ocean.

Is the etheric world to be sought only outside the human being? Obviously not. Through our senses of life, self-movement, and balance, we perceive our own bodily existence in the same way that we perceive outer objects through our senses of smell, taste, and so on. The same interrelationship between an etheric world and an astral being that exists for the outer world must also be possible for when we delve down into our own bodily existence. This means that we must have something within our own bodily inwardness that is equal in nature to the etheric world. In other words, one must carry a piece of this etheric world within oneself as a special "etheric human being." The human entity is thus seen as consisting of three members: the I-being, the astral being, and the etheric being.

Now, it is this etheric human being, imperceptible to the senses, that underlies our perception when we perceive the condition of our own physical existence by means of the first three senses. When this happens, an interplay between the astral and the etheric being takes place. Real-life observation shows that in our mimicry, physiognomy, gestures, and so on, even the I-being leaves an imprint on our outer physical existence. How can it do that? It has been shown that these forces of an inner being work on the form of our outer physical existence and complete their development at sexual maturity. If the I-being is to have an effect on our outer physical nature, it can only do so indirectly by means of this inner human being. Since this effect does occur, the I-being must have an influence on *this* inner human being. This inner being's connection to the astral being is a much more intimate one than its connection to the I-being. This is demonstrated by the fact that how the astral being relates to the outer world is much more strongly expressed in our physical existence than is the I-being's soul content. If someone follows all the events of the outer world with passionate involvement, this is much more evident in his or her physical existence than is the experience that person has of one thing or another through sensory perception. It follows from this that the astral being works on the inner being that we have characterized.

Here, two realms of forces within the human being contrast with each other. The astral being, which interrelates with the outer etheric world, comes up against the inner human being we have characterized, which contains the shaping forces and the conditions for reproduction. It is not difficult to recognize that their encounter is similar to the interrelationship between the astral being and the etheric world. From this, it clearly follows that the inner being we have characterized is the same as the etheric being already presented from a different perspective. Thus, the etheric being is the bearer of our bodily shaping forces and the conditions of reproduction.

We can now see how the human being and the outer world merge. To begin with, the sense world and the I-being interrelate. This interrelationship is underlain by another that exists between the etheric world and the astral being. The formative forces for outer sensory capabilities, for the sense of smell, taste, and so on, must lie, concealed from the senses, within the etheric world. Toward the inside, the astral being interrelates with an etheric being, and in this interrelationship, the perceptions of the senses of life, self-movement, and balance result. On the other hand, however, the etheric being is active in the configuration of the body and in the conditions for reproduction.

An imprint of the etheric being thus lives in what appears as the external body of the human being, but not in a simple way. Consider the shape of the ear, for example. In its own way, it is shaped from two sides. What is alive in the etheric world behind the world of sound makes it possible for the ear to be the organ of the sense of hearing. But this shaping from the outside must be met by one coming from inside, because the etheric being is active and alive also in the form of the body's organs. The reflection that follows, shows just what the relationship is. The forces of the etheric world cannot, wherever they may disperse, call up an organ of hearing. They cannot do it if what they encounter is a stone. Why not? The stone shows nothing within it that is of the same nature as the etheric being we have characterized. It does not give itself its outer form from within, as does the human being. It also does not reproduce. For the organ of hearing to form itself, what molds hearing in the etheric world must therefore encounter the etheric human being. However, that is not enough. The plant grows and reproduces. If we attribute an etheric being to the human being, we must also attribute an etheric plant to the plant. The plant, however, lacks the interrelationship a human being has between the astral being and the etheric world, as characterized above. In order to build up sensory capabilities, this interplay between the etheric world and the astral human being must insert itself into the encounter between the forces of the etheric world and the etheric human being.

The outer human being is thus a complicated being in its configuration: the way that it manifests itself can only come about because an etheric, an astral, and an I-being stand behind this outer configuration. A fourfold membering of the human being results when we add the outer configuration itself, which will be called the "physical being," to these three members of our being.

A consideration of the senses has led us to recognize the human being as a fourfold being. However, if we take these considerations exactly, we can find in them much that is unsatisfying and leads to further questions.

For example, it has been pointed out that our sensory activity presupposes an interrelationship between an etheric world and the astral being. This astral being comes to meet the impressions of our senses as the inwardness nearest them. How the astral being is constituted is expressed in the nuance that sense experiences take on once they are taken inside, without the I-being influencing them directly. Now we can immediately see that the astral being's experiences are imparted to the etheric being, since we see the formative effect of the astral being's experiences on the physical in physiognomy, gestures, and so on. As far as we can see here, however, this effect is slight. Nothing speaks against the possibility that the etheric being, if it were stimulated more strongly *in the same way*, could express itself with greater force in forming the physical being. However, we must admit that the forces that stimulate the etheric being to form our gestures and physiognomy cannot be the same as the ones that work so strongly on it as to mold the forms of the sense organs. What is contained in the etheric world shows itself to be a twofold entity: one that works on the astral being, and another, which is stronger, that works on the etheric being so that it can mold the forms of the senses.

This shows that something works out of the etheric world itself that is similar to the astral being and acts within the etheric being to stimulate the shaping forces that mold the senses. In that concealed domain, where the etheric world is to be looked for, a role is played by another world that works on the etheric being and is related to the astral being. We will call that part of the etheric world that interrelates with the astral being the etheric world in the narrower sense of the word; the other world to which our reflection has led us will be called the astral world because of its relationship to the astral being. We can thus say that the sense world works on the I-being, the etheric world works on the astral being, and the astral world works on the etheric being.

Since as many sense organs must take shape in the physical being as there are separate sensory domains, we must also distinguish as many different domains of forces in the astral world. These domains of force arouse the corresponding formative forces in the etheric being so that the corresponding sense organs are molded in the physical being. This generally stated fact is, however, subject to numerous variations due to the different characters of the sensory domains. Let us take the sense of smell, for example. Through it, the human being penetrates very little into the interior of a body of substance. Only the outer side of substance presents itself to this sense. Contrast this with the sense of warmth. Through it, the human being penetrates much deeper into the interior of an outer body. We can conclude from this that the organ of the sense of smell must have been built up by weaker forces working from outside and stronger ones working within, while the organ of the sense of warmth must have been built up by stronger forces working from the outside and weaker ones working within.

Taking each of the separate sensory domains in turn, we find a hierarchy with regard to how they were built up from the outside and from the inside. The first three senses—the senses of life, self-movement, and balance—are essentially built up from within; that is, the part of the etheric world that develops into the etheric being is active in building them up. This etheric being shapes the physical body in such a way that it is adapted to the perceptions of these senses. The etheric being can shape it in this way because it has been stimulated to do this by the forces of the astral world. We can see that the building up of the human being as it manifests in these three sensory domains has to do with an interaction between the astral world and the etheric being, which has nothing at all to do with the interplay that takes place between the etheric being and the astral being.

It is different with regard to the senses of smell, taste, sight, warmth, and hearing. The etheric being must manage to build them up in such a way that in the corresponding sensory domains, an interplay between the ether world and the astral being is possible. This means that a force must work out of the astral world onto the etheric human being for each of these senses. These forces, working out of the astral world, bring about in the etheric human being the shaping forces that bring the corresponding senses into function. We can therefore say that in the senses of life, self-movement, and balance, the astral world works together directly with the etheric being, while in the senses of smell, taste, sight, warmth, and hearing, it works in a way that takes the astral being into account in forming the sense organs.

It is different again with regard to the senses of language and concept. Here, a much more direct interaction between the outer world and the astral being is necessary than with the five preceding senses. This direct interaction begins to approximate the one that takes place between the I-being and sensations, which leaves its physical imprint in facial expression and physiognomy. This is why these sensory domains develop only after birth, when the human being can come into contact with the outer world, whereas the formative forces for the other senses are already brought into the world at birth. We are justified in saying that, while the forces for building up the senses of life, self-movement, and balance lie deeply concealed behind the sense world, the forces for the senses of speech and concept lie directly behind the sense world. The forces that serve to build up the senses of smell, taste, sight, warmth, and hearing are found in between.

This relationship becomes outwardly clear in the way anthropology describes the sense organs that are present in the sense-perceptible world, that is to say, those of the physical human being. There are essentially no clearly delineated sense organs that can be described for the first three senses. Only for the sense of balance is there an indication of such an organ in the semicircular canals of the ear. The reason for this is that the corresponding shaping forces for these senses serve the general buildup of the physical being, and this is what is sensed in the corresponding sensory domains. The senses of smell, taste, sight, warmth, and hearing are served by specific organs that have been built into the physical being's general structure, because forces of the outer world play a large part in building them up. Such specific organs are essentially no longer present in the case of the senses of language and concept, because these senses approach the domain where the physical being tends toward the soul qualities of the human being.

The I on the one hand and the sense of touch on the other are not to be reckoned as belonging to the domain of the senses, as has been shown. In a way, however, they form both boundaries of our sensory life. The I takes in sense perceptions and transforms their impressions into soul experiences. These are fully *inner* experiences and cease to belong to sensory life. To the sense of touch, the objects remain wholly *external.* What is experienced of them through the sense of touch are actually inner experiences that have related to what is outside in the world through a hidden judgment. These inner experiences belong to the domains of the senses of life, self-movement, and balance. It is clear that the outer world revealed to us through the sense of touch is the only one that can be called a completely external world, in a certain sense, because, in order to be perceived, it does not need to build any particular sense into the human being. Between this outer world and the human I lie the domains out of which the fourfold human being develops.

However, the differences among the sensory domains require us to make further distinctions among them. In the domains of the senses of life, self-movement, and balance, shaping forces of the etheric being—forces that play themselves out in the physical being—reveal themselves. In the case of these forces, the astral being is not taken into account. We are dealing here with forces that work on the inner physical existence of the human being as if, in a certain respect, the astral being did not exist for them. To take effect, they descend into such hidden depths of human existence that they are out of reach of the astral being. In the fields of the next five senses, forming forces manifest that do take the astral being into account. In the senses of language and concept, forces are apparent that are already very close to what is manifested through the senses. We must thus distinguish: the *sense world*, which reveals itself in the I-being, whose conscious life it shapes; the *etheric world*, which is hidden directly behind this sense world and shapes the astral being; in this etheric world, the *astral world* is concealed, which shapes the etheric being in such a way that it develops the shaping of forces of the physical human being. But we must presuppose still another world behind this astral world, for, as has been demonstrated. . . [gap in the text].

. . . senses of hearing and warmth prove to belong together with the processes of breathing and warming more than the former do with the processes of maintaining and growing. We can recognize, however, that these latter processes, which express themselves in the interior of the body on a more feeling level, belong together with the interior senses of self-movement and balance. The life processes of growing and maintaining work more on the side of the interior senses; the processes of warming and breathing work more on the side of the senses through which the human being opens the gates of his or her life to the outside. Thus, the exterior senses are intensified by the life processes in *one* direction, while the interior senses are intensified in the opposite direction.

This fact can be illustrated with an image. Let us think of the set of the sensory domains as a sphere, with sensory experiences working from its surface. In order to do justice to the contrast between the workings of the external and internal senses, we will imagine an indentation at one place on the sphere so that the interior senses can thus also be imagined on the inside of the sphere. If we also want to illustrate, using this sphere, how the life processes intensify the working of sensory experience in one direction or another, we must imagine the sphere as being elongated in two opposing directions. The life processes such as breathing and warming, which have to do with interior experiences that bring the life process into a relationship with the outer world, work toward one end, while the life processes such as secreting, maintaining, and growing, which reveal themselves in inner experiences, work in the other direction.[1] We can therefore say— speaking symbolically, of course—that the human body is given a spherical configuration through the forces that are manifested in its sense organs; this configuration is then elongated by the life organs.

Now, the two directions that come about in this way are of different value for life. On one side, where breathing, warming, and nourishing appear, life opens up to the outside to renew itself; with the processes of secreting and maintaining it pushes its processes into the actual interior of the body. It thereby, in a way, repeats itself within

---

1. See "Secreting [life process]" on page 204 for a schematic presentation of these relationships. — ED.

itself. Further processes then show that, with growing and generating, something is given that, through its own particular nature, is withdrawn from the direct renewal of life. The forces that act to renew life in breathing and warming no longer flow toward it. Toward the interior of the body—or, better said, running from within outward—finished formations come about that must be subject to dying off. (In the animal kingdom, we see how these formations lose their ability to live and are cast off, as in lower animals shedding their skins. A shedding of this sort takes place constantly, if less noticeably, in the human being. We need only observe how our fingernails grow out from the inside and pass over into ends that are dying off.) The two sides of life that we characterized symbolically above therefore show themselves as a polarity between renewing life and destroying life. [Here the text ends.]

APPENDIX 2

An earlier version of Chapter 6 (page 127 ff.). Presumably, this is the original wording of Chapter 6 before it assumed the form in which it appears in the printed version. The first two sentences of this version are almost word-for-word the same as in the printed version.

Within the experience of the I lies nothing that is incited by a sensory process. On the other hand, the I assimilates the outcomes of the sensory processes into its field of experience, fashioning from them its particular structure of inwardness, the actual "I-human being." Within this I-human being thus lie directions of force that meet in the following way: in a certain sense the I lives out its being toward all sides; its own experience encounters forces from different directions, which appear differently according to the particular sense experiences.

In the experience of the so-called sense of touch, the experience is such that its content remains shut up inside; based on the inner experience of what is approaching from outside, only judgments are made. The I therefore feels justified in assuming that the objects of the sense of touch are of the same nature as the I itself, the only difference being that the same actuality that, as experience of touch, takes place within, works in the opposite direction from outside. This judgment, in fact, more or less underlies all perceptions of touch, whereby its nature as judgment usually remains completely unconscious. The I experiences itself in the opposite fashion. To have a perception of touch, the I must unfold its experience outwardly, but constrain it through contact with the object and then let it return upon itself. The I-experience is only present when the totality of the inner experience can unfold unimpeded—when it fills itself solely with its own nature.

The experiences of the other senses lie somewhere between these two extremes. In the sense of concept, the I's experience is constrained least from outside. This experience is such that, in comparison to the I-experience, it feels subdued. It has lost something of its richness. It has given up something of its own strength. We can now recognize the following: in perceiving a concept, the I gives up something of its own content; this occurs because it feels a force coming toward it. The I, as it were, lets itself stream into this oncoming force. If only this ebbing of the I-experience were to occur, the I would merely feel impoverished in its experience. The oncoming stream of force is a reality, however, and works together with what flows out. The result of their working together is the experience of concept.

Let us now imagine that the two streams of force both flow in the same direction, but that one has been present for a long time when the other joins it. Then the second changes the first, and this change is based on the nature of the second. Through this image, the perception of concept can be illustrated. Let the two streams represent I-experiences. Let the older stream flow in experiences of concept, the more recent one in the human I-experience proper. Their confluence results in a change in the older I-experience. This change then stands as a fact alongside the two I-experiences as a third. If we now see in this change the organ of the perception of concept, the meaning of this allegory appears. Two I-experiences work into each other; the newer one brings about the organ of concept in the older one and, depending on the change that the older one has undergone, the impact of the older one is revealed to the younger one.

The same image can be applied to the sense of language; but we will have to imagine that here the younger I-experience is confronted far more with the change in the older experience than its original character, so that, alongside the older I-experience streaming toward it, the younger experiences the change in the older to a considerable extent. This is even more the case for the sense of hearing. Here, the older I-experience recedes behind the change it undergoes through the impact. In the case of the sense of warmth, the change in the older I-experience is such that the nature of this change is essentially the same as the nature of the newer I-experience itself. The impact is then felt in the younger experience of concept as if something present in the change were also present as an impulse in the younger I-experience. When warmth, coming from outside, flows into the I-experiences proper, it is apprehended in a way that proves it to be of the same nature as the inner experiences of warmth.

It is a different situation with the sense of sight. Here the image of the two streams must be chosen such that the stream representing the younger I-experience itself undergoes a change, alongside the change of the older. After the impact, it is not the I-experiences themselves that act on one another, but rather the changes both have undergone. The younger I-experience sends its own change toward the change of the older. If the change in the older I-experience is as strong as the change in the younger, the older lets something of its nature flow into the younger and vice versa, resulting, in fact, in a balance of a sort between the older and younger I-experiences. This is a way of illustrating the reciprocal relationship between the human being and the outer world that occur in the experiences of the sense of sight.

In the case of the sense of taste, the change in the younger I-experience proves to be stronger than the change in the older one; and the result is, in fact, as if the change in the younger I-experience were resisting that of the older. Only a part of the younger I-experiences flows out, as it were; the rest again steps back into the younger I.

The force of the younger I-experience proves to be even stronger in the sense of smell. It occurs most strongly in the so-called sense of touch. There it retains its full character in the face of the older I-experience and, upon contact, wards off the latter in order to experience its entire contents within itself. In the sense of touch, the human I proper sends out its forces so that they are not changed through contact with the outer world, but experiences them again working back from the opposite direction. Therefore, we can also say that, in the case of the sense of touch, the stream of I-experience flows outward, giving up nothing of itself to the outer world, but re-experiencing its entire content in the direction from outside to inside.

In the sense of smell, the I-experience streams outward, loses a part of its content, and experiences the rest in a state of having been changed by an impression from outside. The I supplies its own content, as changed by the impression from outside, as the experience of smell. In the experience of taste, the I must give up more of its content; the change in, and impression on, its own being is thus experienced more strongly than in the experience of smell. In the experience of sight, the I gives up approximately as much as it receives. In the experience of warmth, the older I-experience proves to be the stronger;

the younger I must give up more than it receives; it thus experiences a different kind of change through having something impressed upon it. This change is not one that is worked upon it from outside, but rather one that it works upon itself from within outward. How this change from within outward proceeds then becomes clear in the sense of hearing. Tone no longer lives in the same outer world where the causes of the sense of taste and smell must be placed. Tone unfolds from within outward. This is even more so for the sense of language, and most of all for the sense of concept. [Text ends at this point.]

APPENDIX 3

This essay is not part of the manuscript of the book, but in content it belongs with Chapter 10, "The Human Form."

Let us imagine that the initial, latent human organization, with all the forces it can contain in the physical world, is taken hold of by a force that proceeds directly from the higher spiritual world; this force works from below upward and would, if working on its own, generate only as much of the human being as bears the I. Let us further imagine that before the thus-constituted human being can come about, this force is taken hold of by other forces that work from back to front. (Actually, this only means that they allow the first force to continue working, but deflect it at a right angle.) These other forces proceed directly from the lower spiritual world. They would consist of the contents of the senses of life, self-movement, and balance. Different as these contents may be, they all have in common that they constitute the I's experiences of its own body in the physical world. In order to experience them, they thus presuppose nothing but one's own bodily existence. They have to be experienced through one's own body in the physical world. They thus work there through the individual bodily nature.

The exact opposites of these three senses are the experiences of the senses of concept, tone, and hearing. The experience of the latter senses must be perceived in such a way that, within them, one's own body is shut out. It is characteristic of these experiences that they are independent of one's own bodily nature. Within these experiences the I must therefore experience something that it can incorporate without deriving it from a bodily existence. At the same time, this "something" must be independent of the organs that mediate these experiences—independent in the same sense as is the I itself. In concept, tone, and sound, therefore, there is something that joins the bodily nature proper within the physical world in the same way that the I itself joins this bodily nature. Within human physical nature, latent organs must therefore assert themselves without first having this bodily nature as their prerequisite. These then constitute a particular organism that, within the physical world, comes into contact with the contents of the senses of balance, self-movement, and life, without first coming into contact with the other organs. These contents must therefore work in such a way that they create life-filled organs in an already-existing organism. They are thus forces that, *within the physical world*, reveal the nature of the lower spiritual world as the I itself reveals the nature of the higher spiritual world. The contents of these senses must ray directly into the physical world, just as the I rays into it directly.

When these forces thus work on the physical human being, inasmuch as it is the bearer of the I, they will divide this physical human being into two physical members, one of which consists of dispositions for life that go on to form physical organs of life; while the other will form these dispositions for life in such a way that they can become the bearers of experiences in the I that proceed from the lower spiritual world, just as the I itself proceeds from the higher. These experiences are, however, directly related to the character of the I itself: the experience of concept, tone, and sound. If we now imagine that the contents of the senses of life, self-movement, and balance are the forces that work out of the lower spiritual world from back to front to take hold of the original disposition for the physical body as bearer of the I and impress their own nature upon it, then they would have to imprint into it the organs, through which the I has experiences that thereby bring it into relationship with the lower spiritual world, just as it is in relationship with the higher spiritual world through itself. In their content, sound, tone, and concept are such direct revelations of the lower spiritual world, just as the I is a revelation of the higher spiritual world.

Let it now be further imagined that the original disposition for I of the physical human being is not something at rest within itself, but striving from below upward. Then this disposition would be further fashioned by the content lying in the senses of life, balance, and self-movement into the experiences of sound, tone, and concept through being taken hold of by these contents and being permeated by them in the direction from back to front.

If it is assumed that this physical human disposition, thus transformed, were then to be taken hold of from right to left by the contents of the senses of sight, taste, smell, warmth, and hearing, then these obviously could not act on the disposition if no corresponding dispositions for these senses were present. However, substance itself could, in a way, impinge on this disposition; in latent organs—which through the contents of the senses of balance, self-movement, and life would otherwise develop into organs for concept, tone, and sound—the disposition would thereby turn into those organs that experience the outer effect of substance in themselves. This is possible in the physical world only when organs of life exist.

Now, it is clear that the processes of breathing, warming, and nourishing are possible only through already existing organs of life. In contrast, the processes of secreting, maintaining, growing, and generating call forth I-experiences in the physical world that are not influenced by outer processes of this physical world. To the extent that these life processes reveal themselves in the senses of life, self-movement, and balance, they only presuppose inner organs of life. Life organs thus exist that incorporate into the I without influence from outer substance, just as concept, tone, and sound incorporate themselves into the

I from the physical world. For the experience of the senses of warmth, sight, and taste, outer substances must exist from which the I disengages its experience. Thus life processes exist that are only sensed inwardly; and experiences of warmth, sight, and taste are incorporated into the I as sensations disengaged from the outer substances.

Let it now be assumed that the I, as it lives in the physical world, were to be related to the astral world in the same way that it is related to the higher spiritual world through itself, and to the lower spiritual world through concept, tone, and sound. This can be the case only if it were to have inner life processes within itself that are enkindled by other life processes in such a way that a corresponding outer life process would stimulate an inner life process. It then suffices to recognize generating, growing, maintaining, and secreting as those life processes that can also be stimulated from outside, and breathing, warming, and nourishing as those that can also be stimulated from within. However, at the same time it would have to be assumed that inner breathing, warming, and nourishing are associated with processes that stimulate processes directly in the I from the outer world, just as sound, tone, and concept incorporate them directly into the I. That means: the disposition for I must be affected by the astral world in a way that disengages life processes from life processes in the same sense that the I disengages sound, tone, and concept, and indeed, I-perception, from itself. If inner breathing, warming, and nourishing were stimulated by an I that receives directly from the astral world what is disengaged in the experience of taste, sight, and warmth from the I living in the physical world, then such an I could act as described above. The physical human being would therefore have to encounter an I from the astral world that, by its nature, does not exist *outside* of the experience of taste, sight, and warmth—organs for their perception are needed first—but rather, in its nature, would itself be *inside* these experiences. Experiences of taste, sight, and warmth would have to be imagined, not in the manner of dead matter, but as being ensouled by this I that is related to the higher and lower spiritual worlds. Then such an I could let its inner life act on the physical disposition of the human being; and the experiences of taste, sight, and warmth would radiate through this physical disposition from within. If the contents of these sense experiences were then to penetrate the physical disposition for the I, they could call forth a transformation in those latent organs that bring about the life processes for the senses of balance, self-movement, and life. This would transform these latent organs into organs for generating, growing, maintaining, and secreting. If, therefore, the I were *external* to the physical human disposition up to a certain point in time, from this point on it could stimulate those organs that are on the way to becoming organs of breathing, warming, and nourishing to become organs of secreting, maintaining, growing, and generating.

If the I that radiates experiences of taste, sight, and warmth out of the astral world into the physical world is now imagined not to be at rest in itself, but as striving from left to right, then life organs would come about that, toward the right, would develop as organs of breathing, warming, and nourishing, and toward the left, as organs of secreting, maintaining, growing, and generating. Since the living I, as presupposed, is present in these organs, it would not take the processes of these organs passively, but would dwell in its processes; these would simultaneously be I-experiences. The approach of substance from the left in the organs of nourishing would correspond to maintaining from the right; warming from the left would correspond to growing from the right, breathing from the left with generating—which would be exhalation in this case—from the right. Secreting would hold substance in balance from both sides.

The reversed processes would have to take place when nourishing, warming, and breathing work from the right; then maintaining, growing, and generating would come about from left to right.

Now it is clear that freely hovering experiences of taste, sight, and warmth cannot be present in the physical world to the extent that substance is clearly present, which not only serves breathing, warming, and nourishing, but can be experienced by an I through mere contact, in pure soul experiences. This is the case when substance itself appears as image sensation; desire and impulses for movement link up with image sensation. Thus substance can appear only for the sense of smell. Now, when the substance impinging outwardly upon the latent physical human being is inwardly faced with desire and the impulse to move, simply its impact onto the latent physical human being can entail an image sensation; when this image then releases, through desire, an inner impulse for movement, then a newly forming breathing organ can be arrested in its formative development, but it can also be led beyond the level of its own forces of formative development. If the impulse for movement is stronger than the desire, it continues to develop into an outer organ of breathing; ...[2] if the desire is stronger, then ... if the desire and the impulse for movement are equally strong, then the image sensation, to which it is subjected on its boundary through the impact of substance, confronts its own original disposition from below upward.

However, the I that emanates from the astral world no longer works from below upward, because it characteristically works on the human being only in directions lying in the horizontal plane. Then the only force that can be in an upward direction would be the force that initially worked out of the higher spiritual world from above downward, and the latent senses and life organs that were formed previously and were not taken hold of in the movement from right to left and left to right, because, through the position they attained prior to the action of the astral I, they could not experience any of this I's influences in the above direction that would have led to their completion. These could only be organs for sound, tone, and concept in the process of formation. These organs would not have been completed by the movement from back to front because the force working from above downward restrained their completion.

---

2. For an alternate version of the rest of this section, beginning with this sentence, see page 201.

Assuming that only the contents of the senses of balance, self-movement, and life are active in the movement indicated here, the only interactions to develop could be between the upward-working, latent physical human being and the I itself, working from above downward, and related to the higher spiritual world; furthermore, between these latent senses and the I, which is related to the lower spiritual world, working from front to back. This latter I could itself then come into interaction with what can be self-experience for the I in the senses of balance, self-movement, and life. Since inner organs are now present in the latent physical human being, so ... [At this point the text ends.]

. . . . .

Alternate version of page 200:

... If the desire and impulse for movement are equally strong, then the image sensation, to which it is subjected on its boundary through the impact of substance, confronts its own original direction from below upward.What would then come into consideration for the subsequent processes would be the forces of the I related to the higher and lower spiritual worlds and to the astral world; furthermore, those of the senses of hearing, tone, and concept still in process of formation, which have so far resisted the astral I working in the horizontal plane. Only now do they finally become subject to its influence. They could only develop further through inner life processes that are subjected to the image sensations, desires, and impulses for movement of the I that relates to the astral world in such a way that the completion [of the organ] occurs up to the limit of what is possible when the movement is completed, or the completion is held back before it has reached this limit. The first would occur if the effect of the I related to the astral world on the disposition of the physical human being were to be exhausted in the very moment that the movement from front to back ceases. The second would occur if the effect of this I persists after the completion of the movement. The first is the case for the organ of hearing, in which the I's image sensation brings the formation to a close; the second instance is realized in the senses of tone and concept, which are not led up to the surface of the latent physical human organization, but are held back in its interior. They therefore remain capable of development even after cessation of the movement.

The interaction between the original direction from above downward of the I related to the higher spiritual world, and the striving from below upward of the latent physical human being, now shows itself in the upright stature. In the latter is manifest that the I itself has the same direction as the latent physical human being, so that the forces working from back to front and front to back and those working from left to right and right to left are not the only ones active; rather, the latent physical human being orients itself upward in the wake of the I . . .

The processes that have been indicated here correspond to the image of the human form, as well as to the human course of life. . . [Text ends at this point.]

APPENDIX 4

These notes have been included in this volume because Rudolf Steiner specifically designated them as belonging to Anthroposophy.

The perception of another human being is image sensation; as actuality, opposed to this, stands the fulfillment of what the sense of touch gives, so that, in this inwardness, the reality is given wherein the sense of touch is grounded.

In the perception of concept from the outer world, something is given that, as actuality in the physical bodily nature, has to be regarded as the sense organ of *in-formation*.[3] The concept *lives* in this sense organ. Thus, a life organ is given the form of the organ of concept *from outside*. Behind the life organ is the formative concept: the sense of life.

In the perception of tone from the outer world, something is given that, as actuality in the physical bodily nature, has to be regarded as the sense organ of *tone-formation*. The tone *lives* in this sense organ. Behind the life organ is the formative tone: the sense of self-movement.

In the perception of sound from the outer world, something is given that, in the actuality of the physical bodily nature, has to be regarded as the sense organ of *sound-formation*. The sound comes to perception in this sense organ. In this organ is active, before being the organ of hearing, the sense of balance.

---

3. *Ein-Bildung* in original text. — TRANS.

A. *Life organs* that bring the states of the soul to manifestation in the physical world: on one side.
B. *Life organs* that transform themselves into sense organs: on the other side.

1: The entire organism:
   I-consciousness: the form of the head
2: The blood circulation:
   strivings/desires: fantasy
3: The muscle organism:
   impulses for movement: language

The I lives initially in its soul states, then in life processes, and the perceptions of the outer world are imprinted into these.

Secreting [life process]

Disposition for hearing
Disposition for the
       warmth sense   maintaining   disposition
                            warming   for sight
Disposition for sight   growth

                                             disposition
Disposition for taste   nourishing   for taste
Disposition for smell
Balance

Secreting

APPENDIX 5

These pages constitute an independent and unfinished treatment of their subject and are reprinted here because they are so similar in tone to the content of this volume. They contain an epistemological study based on the senses of language and hearing.

From the I-experience it can be recognized that the human entity works from within to fashion an organism that can, within itself, make immanent the image of an equal yet separate I. What fashions itself into such an organism can be considered as the archetype of an organ of perception. Now the inner constitution of this organism, its law-governed nature, is lost to direct view within the sense world. It is lost to view in the depths of the interweaving activity of soul life and organic life. We become aware of this organism only when we apply it to perceiving the sense world.

When in the midst of immediate sensory life, we do not at first even pay attention to the activity we perform when we turn the content of a perception into I-experience. In order to know something about this activity, we must turn our I away from the content of the perception and direct it toward our own activity. In doing this, we become able to discover soul processes that we carry out at the same time the perception is present as an experience in our I.

These soul processes already do not actually belong to the experiences of consciousness that we have in everyday life. Investigators of the soul find themselves obliged to distinguish between experiences based on confronting the outer world and those based on perceiving our own soul life. If we confront an external object or fact, we can continue to observe it with the same instruments of cognition we first use to perceive it. A soul phenomenon, however, is already over when we attempt to make it the focus of cognition through our observation. This state of affairs has been well described by Franz Brentano in his *Psychology*, where he strongly emphasizes that the inner perception of soul processes can never become inner *observation*.[4]

Objects that we perceive outwardly (as we are in the habit of putting it) *can* be observed; in order to grasp the phenomenon exactly, we turn our full attention to it. But with objects we perceive inwardly, this is completely impossible. This is especially unmistakable in the case of certain psychological phenomena such as, for example, anger. Obviously, the anger burning within us must have already abated if we were to attempt observing it, and thus the object of our observation would have disappeared. The same impossibility exists, however, in all other cases.

---

4. Steiner is referring to Brentano's *Psychologie vom Empirischen Standpunkt*, volume 1, 1874, pp. 35–36. Brentano (1838-1917) was an influential German philosopher who wrote on psychology, ethics, logic, Aristotle, etc. His "intentionalism" influenced Husserl, the creator of phenomenology, while his work on *being* influenced Husserl's student, Martin Heidegger. Freud was also briefly his student. For Steiner's assessment of Brentano, see *Vom Seelenrätsel* (*The Riddles of the Soul*, partially translated as *The Case for Anthroposophy*). — ED.

Because Brentano strictly limits himself within his treatment to what is accessible to ordinary consciousness within the sense world, an important distinction escapes his attention: the distinction between the perception of soul phenomena that occur *due to* perceptions of the outer world, and those that are *fused into* these perceptions of the outer world. Within the sense world, we can perceive the joy or sorrow we may have due to certain perceptions, but not the soul processes that run their course while our I is fully given over to perceiving the outer world. These soul processes are not present before perception occurs, and, as soon as the perception is over, they disappear as far as ordinary consciousness is concerned. This is because our ordinary inner perception extends only to soul processes involving inner experiencing that is not wholly given over to the outer world.

The soul processes that occur while the I is completely absorbed in an object do not lie in the world in which that object lies. With objects in the sense world, these processes lie in a supersensible world. Perceiving such soul processes becomes possible only when the I makes use of totally different capabilities than the ones available to it in the sense world. The I must be able to direct its cognitive capacity to processes that begin when we focus our attention on a sense object, and disappear when this attentiveness ceases.

At this point it should simply be pointed out that this kind of perceiving is possible. To engage in it, the I must totally extricate itself from the realm of the sense world and must be able to contemplate the structure of soul activities that take place while it is absorbed by an outer object in everyday life. The I would have then shifted itself into a supersensible world, in which it would perceive the soul activities that otherwise disappear from consciousness. We only want to mention how the taking up of specific soul exercises makes it possible for the I to shift out of its usual experiences. (To learn about such soul exercises, see my book *How to Know Higher Worlds*.)

Perceiving the corresponding soul processes, therefore, belongs to a supersensible world. However, thinking that remains within the sense world must also be able to infer such processes, since the sense world points to them as surely as smoke points to fire, even if we do not see the fire itself. (This comparison of Herbart's is quite apt.)[5]

According to what has been said above, it seems that ordinary consciousness, active in the sense world, can at most acknowledge the supersensible world that has been described, but that it must necessarily be denied access to any more precise insight into it. This would indeed be the case unless something could appear in this realm of consciousness that can present the soul's inner activity and the perception of an object to our awareness at the same time. Precisely what would the nature of this "something" have to be? Not only would the experience of a perception

---

5. Johann Friedrich Herbart, 1776-1841, philosopher, psychologist, and educator. Complete works in 12 volumes. It has not yet been possible to trace this comparison. Using the same comparison, Rudolf Steiner also mentions Herbart in *The Riddles of Philosophy*, Anthroposophic Press, Spring Valley, NY, 1973, pp.185 ff. — ED.

have to be present within the sense world, but we would also have to be able to turn our attentiveness to this experience in a way that lets us perceive our own activity during the experience. In the domain of sensory experiences, this is possible to a somewhat limited extent in our relationship to our own speaking. However, hearing our own phonetic tones with our ears is not what is meant, because hearing our own phonetic tones differs in no way from hearing the tones of others. It only brings about a sense perception. We must rather turn our attention to the dim consciousness we can have of the movements of our organs of speech when a tone is to be brought forth. If this consciousness were not present, we could never attain the power necessary to produce a particular phonetic tone.

What, then, is present in the soul when a phonetic tone is produced? In addition to the tone itself, which belongs to the sense world, an image of the movement of the corresponding organs is present.

This image is in no way similar in character to a mental image acquired through outer perception. The latter is the more correct the more it coincides with the perception. But the image of how our speech organs move when a tone is uttered cannot coincide with the tone itself. Indeed, a human being may never bring this image to consciousness; then the self-movements required for speech will simply always be carried out unconsciously. However, deep within the organism of such an unaware speaker, the same thing must be taking place that takes place in someone who penetrates ever deeper into the speech organism and thus raises the configuration of the organs of phonetic tone up into consciousness in image form. The speaker's knowledge of the latter does not, of course, call into being the reality of what is perceived. What is perceived is a soul process that takes place concurrently with the sensory phenomenon of intonation.

In the speech process, this soul process, however, is more or less covered up because the I is absorbed in the spoken intonation. Under these circumstances, specific exercise is required to turn our attention to our organism's self-movement. Now, perceiving self-movement while speaking is not essentially different from perceiving the self-movement that takes place when we lift a leg or move an arm. But since no tone is voiced in these movements, there can be no question of outer perception. That we may also see our own movements, for example, is of no consequence for what lives in the soul as the perception of self-movement.

When we are absorbed in the perception of self-movement, a soul process occurs like those that must that take place concurrently with an outer perception. But, with these soul processes, the perception of a process corresponding to outer perception remains at first completely outside our ordinary consciousness. Only a soul process comes to consciousness; what is actually going on in the body while this soul process is taking place cannot directly become an object of consciousness.

In the sense of what has been presented here, it seems justified to conclude that in the case of outer perceptions, the content of what is perceived becomes conscious, while the corresponding soul processes remain concealed; in the case of the perception of the organism's inner processes, these processes themselves do not become directly evident, but the corresponding soul processes do appear in our consciousness.

On the basis of this conclusion, we can gain an idea of the nature of these two types of perceptions. In outer perceptions, the content of the perception rises on the horizon of consciousness, while below this horizon a stimulus that does not rise into consciousness plays upon the human being. This stimulus is of the same type as, for example, the soul process that enters into consciousness in the case of the organism's self-movement. If, in the corresponding case, outer sense perception could remain unconscious while the I could absorb itself completely in the inner soul process, the I would have to experience something similar to self-movement. However, in this case it would find no inner process causing the soul process.

Let us take another look at the process of hearing a phonetic tone. Let us, however, imagine that we are listening not to our own speech, but to the speech of another human being. The movement of our speech organs and thereby the I's activity in our own organism are, in this case, absent. The other's I takes the place of our own; its activity produces the tone. Present in the listener is the above-characterized soul process that doesn't come to consciousness. Since it is present, however, it does confront the tone. The tone encounters the resistance of the soul process and is thereby raised to consciousness. We must now simply imagine that the I interweaves itself with the tone after the latter is arrested by the soul process, and we will have an idea of how the tone becomes conscious. It is the reverberation of the tone on our own soul process that comes to consciousness in our I. In this case, the tone first lives with the speaker; then it is thrown back by the listener's own soul process; after having been thrown back, it lives in the listener. If we realize how the tone in question is essentially present in the same way in both speaker and listener, imagining it becoming conscious in the way described here will present no difficulties. And it then seems quite evident that in hearing tone voiced by a speaking human being, the conscious I is present, not within, but outside its own unconscious soul processes present in tone perception.

Let us now compare this to perceiving a sound that proceeds from a lifeless body. The conscious I is interwoven with this sound in exactly the same way it is interwoven with the external tone. It must therefore become conscious in the same way. A soul process must offer resistance to the sound, and the sound captured in this way must then be incorporated into the I.

This is what the process looks like when it is compared with the perception of a tone. However, if we look at it from the realm of the sense-perceptive world, scruples arise with regard to such a view. In this world of perception, the starting-point of the sound is a body whose parts are in motion in a particular way. We become aware that this movement continues into the air. The air that has been set in motion reaches the ear; as a result of the air's movement beating against the ear and the nerve organism, the sound comes about in the I-consciousness. One can now easily arrive at the idea that absolutely nothing is present in the outer world except the movement of the body in question and the movement of the air, and that the sound itself comes about within the soul only as a response to the physical movement. This idea is so tempting that it lives as a belief in many philosophical worldviews. It is then extended to all sense perceptions, so that it is said that sound, light, and so on, are present only within the human soul; the world outside it is silent and dark.

We should not have unquestioned faith in this idea because of the perception of tone of a speaking human being. In this case, there is no doubt that the tone heard is in essence identical to the tone that is spoken. To say that the speaker's tone is carried to the listener by the stream of outer mediators is thus no mere picture, but certainly corresponds to the actual process; in what the listener perceives is a true counterpart of what is present in the outer world, not merely a soul response to a sound-less outer process.

Here too an objection is possible. One could say the following: the speaker causes certain movements of his or her organs of speech and therefore also of the air. Outside of the speaking being there is, however, nothing present except these movements in the air. Because of the particular character of these movements, the response that comes about in the listener's soul indeed corresponds to the process through which the speaker produced the movement. This objection, however, is not relevant. The issue here is whether that which is eventually brought about in the I has any reality as such outside of the I. And this is undoubtedly so when a spoken tone is heard.

Now the connection the I makes with a sound that proceeds from a lifeless body is no different from the connection it makes with the tone of a speaking being. Therefore, we can think no differently about the outer or inner existence of a sound with regard to the whole human organism than we do about the existence of a phonetic tone.

The objective existence of a tone is in the speaker. The listener relates the tone to this speaker. In what way does this happen? Certainly in that the listener connects the tone with the immediate impression—this tone proceeds from a being of my own kind. If someone were certain of being in a room devoid of other human beings, and if a tone were to emanate from some corner, he or she would obviously not relate the tone to a speaking human being. In addition to the perceptions of tone, other perceptions play a role in bringing about a relation of this kind. Now these other perceptions are certainly not, for example, the visual perceptions that we receive from the speaker's form, but rather everything that makes us arrive at the judgment: the speaker is a being like myself, and that the cause of the voiced tone lies within this being, as it can similarly lie within myself. The process through which we arrive at this judgment is a very complicated one and is lost in the multiplicity of experiences through which we come to recognize entities of our own kind in other human beings. When the I finds itself interwoven with a tone, the result of all such experiences is, however, the basis for associating this tone to an entity of our own kind.

Arriving at the conclusion that "a human being is speaking" seems simple to naive consciousness, but is actually the result of very complicated processes. These processes culminate in concurrently perceiving within a tone, in which you experience *yourself*, another I. During this experience, everything else is disregarded; and—inasmuch as we turn our attention to it—we are focused on the connection from I to I. The whole mystery of *empathy* with the I of another is expressed in this fact. If this fact is to be described, this cannot be done without saying: we sense our own I in the I of the other. If we then perceive a tone coming from the other I, our own I lives in that tone, and therefore in the other I.

Now, if our I lives interwoven with a sound coming from a lifeless object, the only sensory object to which it can relate the sound is this lifeless object. If the I approaches the object, however, it finds that it cannot live within the object initially, as it can live in another I through tone. It is interwoven with the sound, but not with the lifeless object. However, observation of the sense world does demonstrate a relationship between the lifeless object and the organ of hearing (and the corresponding nerve organism). But the same relationship also exists between the speech organism of a speaker and the ear and nerve organism of the listener. Yet in the latter case the relationship signifies only a mediating stream for the tone that is objectively present in the speaker's I. This relationship therefore does not suggest that in it is to be found the objective reality of a lifeless object's sound, and that the perceived content of the sound is only a response on the part of the human soul. The only possibility is to think that also in this case the I is bound up with the sound just as it is with the tone. In the sense of what was presented above, then, a lifeless sound would have to confront the listener, the soul processes we have described would have to originate below the horizon of consciousness, and the I would then live in the sound, because the latter encounters its resistance in the corresponding soul processes. The sound would then have to be present in the outer world just as the tone is present in the speaker—the difference being that no reason would exist that could induce the listening I to relate the sound from a lifeless object to a being of its own kind. This can only mean that in the case of human tone, the listener imparts his or her I to the I of another, while in the case of a sound from a lifeless object, the I is imparted only to the sound itself. The listening I feels induced to penetrate through the phonetic tone, but not through the sound from the lifeless object. In other respects both tone and lifeless sound belong to the sense world in the same way, and the listening I is linked with both in the same way. For this reason, the relationship of sound to what takes place as air movements, and so on, between the sounding object and the listening human being must not be thought of as any different from the relationship of tone to the corresponding outer movement.

The sound must thus be brought into a relationship to the outer lifeless object that is similar to the tone's relationship to the speaking human being. This cannot happen without relating the lifeless object to an inner life of its own. This will present certain difficulties as long as we consider the lifeless object as a self-contained entity. Conceiving of it in this way, however, would be similar to considering the human larynx as a self-contained entity. In order for the larynx to produce a tone or a sound, it must be in connection with the speaker's processes of soul and I. In the sense world, these processes of soul and I cannot be examined from outside. They are supersensible processes. Only those aspects of the human being that are sense-perceptible may be considered as belonging to the sense world. The tone belongs to the sense world; its soul content does not. What can be observed in the sense world as the movement of a sounding, lifeless body—as air movements and so on—must be thought of as effects, within the sense world, of what lives in the sound. Inasmuch as the sound, as perceived by the I, cannot itself be taken to be the cause of a movement, we must assume the existence of a supersensible world in which sound is based, and that generates the movement wherein the nonliving manifests itself as sound to the I. The connection that an I, through the human tone, establishes within the sense world to a being of its own kind, must, in the case of sound, be sought in a supersensible world lying behind the sound.

When a singing human being produces a sound, we can distinguish, first, the sound that is finally heard by the I: it belongs to the sense world; second, the soul movement (soul process) in which the sound is based. The latter cannot be observed in the sense world, but belongs to a supersensible world of which the human being is aware only because the human being lives in this world. [Here text ends.]

BIBLIOGRAPHY

- Learning to breathe properly.

  The Foundations of Human Experience, Anthroposophic Press, Hudson, NY, 1996; previously published as *The Study of Man*. first lecture, Aug. 21, 1919.

- The twelve senses.

  Ibid. eighth lecture, Aug. 29, 1919.

- The theme of the senses: ten senses.

  The Wisdom of Man, of the Soul and of the Spirit; also titled, *Anthroposophy, Psychosophy, and Pneumatosophy* (out of print; newly translated and republished in 1996 as *Spiritual Psychology*. Anthroposophic Press, Hudson, NY), lecture, June 27, 1909.

- How the I lives in the world through the twelve senses.

  Toward Imagination: Culture and the Individual. Anthroposophic Press, Hudson, NY,1990. third lecture, June 20, 1916.

- The realms of the twelve senses and the seven life processes.

  The Riddle of Humanity: The Spiritual Background of Human History. Rudolf Steiner Press, London, 1990. first lecture, July 29, 1916.

- The relationship of the senses to thinking, feeling, and willing.

  Man as a Being of Sense and Perception. Steiner Book Centre, North Vancouver, Canada, 1958. first lecture, July 22, 1921.

- The zodiac and the realms of the twelve worldviews.

  Human and Cosmic Thought. Rudolf Steiner Press, London, 1961. third lecture, Jan. 22, 1914.

- The thinking or concept sense.

  In the 1918 appendix to *Intuitive Thinking as a Spiritual Path: A Philosophy of Freedom.* Anthroposophic Press, Hudson, NY, 1995. The primary subject of this *basic book* by Rudolf Steiner is the development of thinking for perception, leading to spiritual freedom.

- The sense of smell.

  The Evolution of the Earth and Man, and the Influence of the Stars: 14 Lectures to the Workmen, Anthroposophic Press, Hudson, NY, 1987; Lecture IX, August 9, 1924.

- At the portals of the senses, feelings and aesthetic judgment.

  Spiritual Psychology: Anthroposophy, Psychosophy, and Pneumatosophy, lecture of November 3, 1910.

- The child as a sense organ.

  Soul Economy and Waldorf Education. Anthroposophic Press, Hudson, NY, 1986. seventh lecture, Dec. 29, 1921.

- The soul imitating the surroundings.

  The Child's Changing Consciousness and Waldorf Education. Anthroposophic Press, Hudson, NY, 1988.

- The will in each sense organ.

  Ibid.

  The Foundations of Human Experience (The Study of Man).

- Imitating the spiritual in the physical.

  A Modern Art of Education. Rudolf Steiner Press, London, 1972.

- The eye as an example: less of a sense organ in the third and fourth year.

  The Kingdom of Childhood. Anthroposophic Press, Hudson, NY, 1995.

- Sense organs and fantasy.

  Ibid.

- The individual senses.

  Practical Advice to Teachers. Rudolf Steiner Press, London, 1976.

DURING THE LAST TWO DECADES of the nineteenth century the Austrian-born Rudolf Steiner (1861–1925) became a respected and well-published scientific, literary, and philosophical scholar, particularly known for his work on Goethe's scientific writings. After the turn of the century he began to develop his earlier philosophical principles into an approach to methodical research of psychological and spiritual phenomena.

His multifaceted genius has led to innovative and holistic approaches in medicine, science, education (Waldorf schools), special education, philosophy, religion, economics, agriculture (Biodynamic method), architecture, drama, new arts of eurythmy and speech, and other fields. In 1924 he founded the General Anthroposophical Society, which today has branches throughout the world.